T0383812

Cambridge Elements ≡

Elements in Decision Theory and Philosophy
edited by
Martin Peterson
Texas A&M University

RATIONALITY AND TIME BIAS

Abelard Podgorski
National University of Singapore

Shaftesbury Road, Cambridge CB2 8EA, United Kingdom

One Liberty Plaza, 20th Floor, New York, NY 10006, USA

477 Williamstown Road, Port Melbourne, VIC 3207, Australia

314–321, 3rd Floor, Plot 3, Splendor Forum, Jasola District Centre,
New Delhi – 110025, India

103 Penang Road, #05–06/07, Visioncrest Commercial, Singapore 238467

Cambridge University Press is part of Cambridge University Press & Assessment,
a department of the University of Cambridge.

We share the University's mission to contribute to society through the pursuit of
education, learning and research at the highest international levels of excellence.

www.cambridge.org
Information on this title: www.cambridge.org/9781009517133

DOI: 10.1017/9781009216920

When citing this work, please include a reference to the DOI 10.1017/9781009216920

First published 2024

A catalogue record for this publication is available from the British Library.

ISBN 978-1-009-51713-3 Hardback
ISBN 978-1-009-21693-7 Paperback
ISSN 2517-4827 (online)
ISSN 2517-4819 (print)

Rationality and Time Bias

Elements in Decision Theory and Philosophy

DOI: 10.1017/9781009216920
First published online: November 2024

Abelard Podgorski
National University of Singapore

Author for correspondence: Abelard Podgorski, phiap@nus.edu.sg

Abstract: We often care not only about what happens to us, but when it happens to us. We prefer that good experiences happen sooner, rather than later, and that our suffering lies in our past, rather than our future. Common sense suggests that some ways of caring about time are rational, and others are not, but it is surprisingly challenging to provide justifying explanations for these tendencies. This Element is an opinionated, nontechnical guided tour through the major arguments for and against different kinds of so-called time bias.

Keywords: time bias, rationality, future bias, near bias, diachronic rationality

ISBNs: 9781009517133 (HB), 9781009216937 (PB), 9781009216920 (OC)
ISSNs: 2517-4827 (online), 2517-4819 (print)

Contents

Introduction

There is a movie I am eagerly anticipating – the first film by my favorite director to be released in a decade, finally scheduled for release in a few months. I open the paper, and read some devastating news. Due to a strike, the release schedule has been pushed back – I will not be able to see it for at least a year. I am crestfallen. But life goes on, and I wait patiently. Finally, the release date approaches, and I get more and more excited. Of course, I buy tickets on the first night the movie is showing, even though the seats I manage to get are not as good as they would have been if I'd waited another week for the crowds to thin, and even though I must decline an otherwise exciting invitation to attend. I sit and watch, and it is everything I hoped for and more. And yet my feeling walking out of the theater is bittersweet. That experience, wonderful though it was, is gone now, receding into the past. I can watch the movie again, of course, but it will never be quite the same – some effects are lost without the element of surprise. I am jealous of my friends who haven't seen it yet. My life seems a bit emptier now that it is all in my past rather than my future.

Not everyone is a cinephile, of course, and so the details vary, but experiences like this are as common as they are philosophically mysterious. Both my emotional tango and my practical decision-making around my theatrical experience are driven by a deep concern not just for how good the experience will be, but *when* it will be – whether it will be sooner rather than later, and whether it is future rather than past. And yet while responding to time in this way is completely natural, if we start to question our *justification* for it, we may find ourselves at a loss. Why be disappointed when the release date is pushed back, if I'm going to see it eventually either way? Why buy tickets for the first night, if the movie would be just as good a week later and I'd avoid the downsides? Why be sad that it is in the past rather than the future, if in either case I am not experiencing it now? Why is the future being empty of that experience so disheartening, when I never gave a second thought to the past being empty of it?

This Element is about what rationality demands about the way we care about our past, present, and future. It is primarily meant to be a critical survey of the most influential existing attempts both to rationally justify and to criticize agents who care about how their experiences are distributed in time in different ways. Following the literature, we'll call such agents *time-biased*, though this terminology is perhaps unfortunate – we do not want to prejudge the rationality of their attitudes.

Here it is worth clarifying the notion of "rationality" at play in this Element. We will be understanding rationality normatively – someone who is irrational is doing something wrong or making some kind of mistake. This is in contrast to various purely descriptive characterizations of rationality which are sometimes assumed in the economics literature. Beyond this, we will leave the notion deliberately unspecified. A more committal conceptual characterization of rationality, for example as essentially having to do with coherence, or with responsiveness to reasons, is liable to be controversial. Since adjudicating these debates is beyond the scope of our Element, we will remain neutral, but some of the arguments we discuss will have more or less plausibility given specific high-level conceptions of rationality, and we will note this as those arguments come up. Most of the arguments we will consider assume we have some intuitive grip on the sorts of things rationality requires of us, but our intuitions may in particular cases be revisable in light of other conflicting intuitions or theoretical considerations.

Before we begin, to preclude any disappointed expectations, a few words are warranted about related topics which we *won't* cover in this Element. First, we are only interested in *pure* time bias – preferences responding more or less directly to *when* some event occurs. It can be tricky to distinguish an agent with a pure time bias from one who is responding to other factors that happen to correlate with time. For example, it is typically the case that we are more uncertain about the prospect of pleasures that occur far into the future – I am fairly certain that a dinner at my favorite restaurant now will bring me joy, but less certain that a voucher for such a dinner in a year will do so. My tastes might well have changed, or the restaurant might have shut down between now and then. The fact that the prospect of the voucher carries less weight in my decision-making than an immediate dinner might superficially appear like time bias favoring the near future over the far future, but could alternatively be explained by the difference in my confidence in their positive effects. Although discussion by economists or psychologists about time bias often lumps together these different explanations for a preference for immediate gratification, for our purposes it is important to separate them. It is not controversial at all that it is rational to prefer immediate to deferred gratification insofar as this is due to the greater uncertainty of the latter. But the rationality of pure time bias is much more disputed.

A tougher case is that of someone who prefers that their life has an "upward trajectory" – that the good parts of their life happen later rather than earlier. On the one hand, this seems closer to a pure time bias than the uncertainty case above – the placement of their experiences in time does make a difference to whether their desires are satisfied. On the other hand, their preference might be characterized in ways that are temporally neutral – as a preference that their life has a certain narrative structure.[1] It just happens to be the case that their life won't have the relevant structure unless their experiences are organized a certain way in time. By way of comparison, someone who has a strong desire

---

[1] An influential discussion of this issue can be found in Velleman (1991).

to have children with a spouse will only satisfy this desire if they have children *after* they get married. In that respect, it matters quite a bit to them when certain events happen. But this is not what people generally have in mind in discussions of time bias. So here too, we ought to distinguish preferences for particular sequences of events from pure time bias, that is, from preferences for events to occur at certain times *as such*.[2] We will not be considering issues surrounding how the distribution of events in time affects the narrative value of a life.

Second, we will largely be ignoring many interesting *empirical* questions about time bias – about its extent, its psychological explanation, and its usefulness in modeling human behavior. For example, while a tendency to discount future goods in a range of contexts has been shown in a range of studies, how much of this tendency is due to pure time bias rather than other factors (such as the aforementioned greater uncertainty about the future) remains controversial.[3] A quick excuse for not wading into these debates is that the fact that we *are (or are not)* time-biased in a certain way, or for a certain reason, does not immediately bear on whether it is *rational* for us to be time-biased in that way or for that reason – a normative, rather than an empirical question. But this would be a little *too* quick. One might think there should be a presumption in favor of the rationality of widely shared dispositions, in which case the empirical question of whether pure time bias explains the way we discount the future is relevant to the normative case in favor of it. Or it might be that empirical investigation into our intuitive judgments about the rationality of agents who exhibit time bias might make us more or less confident in those intuitive judgments.[4] Insofar as such judgments play a role in justifying our views about rationality, that kind of empirical work also bears on the normative question we are after.[5]

Nevertheless, in this Element we will be simply setting aside the class of arguments that use our own time-biased dispositions or intuitive reactions to cases involving time bias as a direct reason to accept or reject those biases. And we will likewise set aside arguments over whether those intuitive reactions are worth taking seriously as evidence – whether, for example, we have plausible debunking explanations for those intuitions. This is not to say that those

---

[2] For an empirical investigation into preferences about sequences of events, see Loewenstein and Prelec (1993) and Kahneman et al. (1993).

[3] See Frederick et al. (2002) or Ericson and Laibson (2019) for an empirical review from the economic point of view. Żuradzki (2016) considers the philosophical implications of the empirical literature.

[4] Notably, the existing empirical literature does not investigate our intuitions about the rationality of time bias – it is focused on our time biased dispositions themselves and their explanation.

[5] Some of the philosophical literature addresses these psychological questions on the way to normative conclusions along these lines. For example, Latham et al. (2023) argue that there is no psychological asymmetry between the explanation of two different kinds of time bias in order to show that there is no normative asymmetry between them.

arguments cannot provide legitimate reasons – I think they can – but it is an interesting question whether anything can be said in favor of or against such dispositions aside from simply how good or bad they seem to us and how much or little we should trust those seemings. After all, we would like if possible to get an *explanation* of why time biases might be justified, whether in the forms we exhibit them or in some other form.

By bracketing these empirical arguments off, we can avoid getting into the weeds of a complex and active literature which is constantly changing and which is better addressed by psychology than philosophy. That being said, our evaluation of the arguments that try to avoid grounding in our bare intuitions about time bias will turn out to be relatively critical (to spoil things a little). So one lesson that might be taken from this Element is that the direct intuition-grounded arguments are the best we have for settling the disputes in this area, and therefore that the empirical work which might bear on the trustworthiness of those intuitions is even more relevant than one might have thought.

Third, we will, like most of the philosophical literature, be limiting our consideration to *hedonic* time bias – preferences regarding pleasurable and painful experiences. This is in part because plausible views of welfare typically agree that pleasures are good and pains bad for people, while other candidate goods, such as accomplishment or relationships, are more controversial. It is also often assumed that our actual time bias is specific to these hedonic goods.[6] We will further limit the discussion to preferences about agents' *own* pleasurable and painful experiences, to avoid complications arising from an asymmetry between our self-directed and other-directed biases.[7]

I'll add a few notes about the approach I will take. This Element takes the form of a guided tour through major philosophical arguments from the literature – these arguments will be presented and then critiqued. As a guide, I will be opinionated but not especially aligned either with those who defend the rationality of time bias or those who object to it. If there is an overall point of view that comes through, I expect it to be one of general *pessimism* about existing arguments – I will argue that most of the major arguments both against the rationality of various forms of time bias and those in favor of it have serious weaknesses, though some of these are more fatal than others.

I will also be employing practically no formalism and assuming no background. Although discussions of time bias in economics especially are often quite technical, I do not think such an approach is necessary to appreciate the normative, philosophical issues at stake. There are a few relevant mathematical

---

[6] For example, by Caspar (2013) and Dougherty (2015). See Greene et al. (2022) for some research challenging this assumption.

[7] See Hare (2008) for a discussion of this topic.

results which have been proven by others and which will be mentioned here, but we will not go through the proofs ourselves.

The basic structure will have three parts, each considering one species of time bias, in order from the least often defended to the most often defended. For each, we will consider both whether the bias is rationally *permissible,* and whether it might be rationally *required.* With that, let us begin.

Part I: Uncentered Time Bias

To introduce the first kind of time bias, let us consider the following case:

Garfield Hates (Pain on) Mondays

> Garfield prefers pain on any other day to an equal amount of pain on Mondays. This is not because he experiences pain any differently on Mondays – he simply strongly desires not to have the pain then. Prospectively, he will willingly choose to undergo a painful operation without anesthetic next Tuesday rather than have it performed next Monday with anesthetic. Retrospectively, he is relieved to learn that a painful childhood accident he had forgotten happened on a Tuesday rather than a Monday.

This case resembles a case discussed by Parfit (1984) of someone who is indifferent to pain on all future Tuesdays. But that case involves a preference with two salient asymmetries – between some days of the week and other days, and between the future and the past or present. Since each of these is an independent potential source of irrationality, it is worth isolating them, and our case only involves the former. Garfield's preferences reflect what we can call an *uncentered* time bias – uncentered because his attitudes towards different times do not depend on where those times are *relative to the present.* He cares more about pain on Mondays than Tuesdays whether those days are in the past, present, or future. *Centered* time biases, which can only be characterized relative to the time at which the agent has them, will be considered later.

Uncentered time biases are often ignored in the literature, perhaps because it is assumed that these are not the biases exhibited by ordinary humans, or perhaps because they seem so obviously irrational to be not worth discussing. But I think this is a mistake. As we will see, many arguments against other forms of time bias do not carry over to uncentered time bias. If uncentered time bias is obviously irrational, then these other arguments might end up being insufficiently general. The arguments against uncentered time bias, on the other hand, do plausibly generalize to other forms of time bias, meaning those other arguments might also end up being redundant. Moreover, our discussion in this Element will ultimately suggest that the independent arguments against other forms of time bias have serious defects. This suggests a reading of the state of the debate on which the case against time bias of any kind stands and falls with the case against uncentered time bias.

Intuitively, Garfield's attitude is in some way defective. But why? Parfit writes of his similar example that "In these cases the concern is not less because of some intrinsic difference in the object of concern. The concern is less because of a property which is purely positional, and which draws an arbitrary line. These are the patterns of concern that are, in the clearest way, irrational." (125–126)

But making this criticism stick is far from easy. The first part of Parfit's complaint seems to be that concern like Garfield's towards pain on a particular day isn't grounded in the *intrinsic* quality of the pain. But why is this a problem? It does not seem that *in general* it is irrational to care about something more or less because of extrinsic features, even when it is pain or pleasure. That a pain belongs to myself, or to my child, is not an intrinsic feature of that pain and yet it does not seem irrational to care more about it than a stranger's pain for that reason. Part of Parfit's project in *Reasons and Persons* is to argue that we should care less about the boundaries around and between persons, and a devotee of that project might insist that those concerns are indeed irrational. But that is in any case a revisionary view, and so not the ideal thing to appeal to as part of an argument against time bias.

So what is worth focusing on in Parfit's comment is not whether Garfield's concern is due to intrinsic features but whether it is *arbitrary*. Parfit is far from the first or the only thinker to criticize time bias on these grounds.[8]

The Arbitrariness Argument Against Uncentered Time Bias

To condemn Garfield, one might make the following argument:[9]

1) *Nonarbitrariness:* At any given time, a rational agent's preferences are insensitive to arbitrary differences.
2) The uncentered temporal location of experiences is an arbitrary difference between them.
3) An agent who exhibits uncentered time bias has preferences that are sensitive to the uncentered temporal location of experiences.
4) So, uncentered time bias is irrational.

Before we can evaluate *Nonarbitrariness* and the argument, we need to understand what it means for a difference to be arbitrary in the relevant sense. In this normative context, following Sullivan (2018), it is natural to take arbitrariness

---

[8] See for example Sidgwick (1884, 180–381) or more recently Sullivan (2018).

[9] This is a modification of the argument Sullivan (2018) gives against centered time biases.

as a matter of *reasons* – a difference between two things is arbitrary if it does not provide a reason to prefer one over the other.

An initial complication: on this understanding, whether a difference is arbitrary depends on whether *in fact* it provides a reason to prefer one thing over another. A difference can therefore be arbitrary even if an agent *believes* that it provides a reason to prefer one thing over another – indeed, even if the agent reasonably believes that. But philosophers often take rational norms to be sensitive to the way agents (reasonably) believe things to be, rather than the way they are. It can be rational to drink poison, for example, if you reasonably believe it is water. So, it might be argued, whether uncentered time bias is rational for a given agent should depend not on whether temporal location is an arbitrary difference, but on whether an agent reasonably believes that temporal location is an arbitrary difference.[10] And perhaps there is little to say about what any agent whatsoever must rationally believe about their reasons – that will depend on their particular evidence or intuitions.

One might defy this line of argument by positing an asymmetry between the way rationality treats normative beliefs about reasons and nonnormative beliefs (e.g., about whether a drink is poison), a topic of significant dispute in the literature on normative uncertainty.[11] Or one might insist that it is never reasonable to believe false things about normative reasons (perhaps because they are a priori).[12] Alternatively, one might evade it entirely by changing the topic from whether time bias is ever rational to whether it is ever rational from someone who is *fully informed* (including about normative reasons). In what follows, I will ignore this complication.

It might initially seem that *Nonarbitrariness* is obviously false. Some people prefer chocolate ice cream to vanilla, and other people prefer vanilla to chocolate. Surely the difference between chocolate and vanilla doesn't provide a *reason* to prefer one over the other. Does the principle implausibly imply that people who prefer one type of ice cream over the other are irrational?

To see why it does not, we should realize that in the normal case, someone who prefers chocolate to vanilla does so because they *like the taste* of chocolate more than vanilla. And while the difference between vanilla and chocolate might be arbitrary from the point of rationality, the difference between tastes that one likes and those one doesn't is not arbitrary. Something similar will be true of other preferences we often identify as "matters of taste" – preferences

---

[10] Relatedly, Saad's (2023) argument in favor of time bias, discussed later in this section, appeals to claims about agent's reasonable credences about value, rather than the facts about value.

[11] Brian Weatherson (2019) defends the externalist view that denies the significance of beliefs about normative reasons.

[12] Brian Hedden (2016) suggests a view along these lines.

between music or about hair color. So *Nonarbitrariness* is compatible with a certain widely accepted sense in which our rational preferences may be "subjective" or depend on our individual psychology.

Nevertheless, the principle is highly controversial – it is in tension with a number of views about practical rationality. On one influential point of view, there are no reasons for attitudes like intrinsic desire or preferences. Most famously, this view is suggested by David Hume in his *A Treatise of Human Nature* (1739), where he writes:

> Where a passion is neither founded on false suppositions, nor chuses means insufficient for the end, the understanding can neither justify nor condemn it. It is not contrary to reason to prefer the destruction of the whole world to the scratching of my finger. It is not contrary to reason for me to chuse my total ruin, to prevent the least uneasiness of an Indian or person wholly unknown to me. It is as little contrary to reason to prefer even my own acknowledged lesser good to my greater, and have a more ardent affection for the former than the latter. (2.3.3.6)

To litigate the plausibility of the Humean "no reasons for preferences" picture would be an enormous project in its own right and I will not attempt it here. But it is worth noting that the Humean picture is not quite as extreme as it might seem at first. Accepting that there are no reasons for preferences does not require thinking that no preferences, or patterns of preferences, are rationally criticizable at all.

A distinction is often made between *structural* requirements of rationality, which concern our attitudes' internal coherence, and *substantive* requirements, which concern their justification and relationship to our reasons. To escape the arbitrariness argument it is sufficient to reject the latter, and one may still maintain that desires which are self-defeating or inconsistent are irrational for structural reasons. We will later look at arguments against other kinds of time bias that appeal to such structural requirements. While Sullivan (2018) takes *Nonarbitrariness* to represent an "elementary requirement of consistency and coherence" (39), I think this is a mischaracterization. It is not inconsistent to have preferences which are not grounded in reasons, if the contents of those preferences are not in tension with each other. Preferring apples to oranges, oranges to bananas, and bananas to apples is inconsistent. But preferring apples to oranges without a reason to do it is objectionable, if at all, for a very different kind of reason. The purported requirement to desire in accordance with reasons is not a matter of coherence but a demand for substantive justification of our desires. This illustrates an important point: *Nonarbitrariness* fits better with some high-level conceptions of what rationality is all about than others. It is most plausible on a picture which takes rationality to be about properly responding to one's reasons (though it is not immediately entailed by such a view). But it is less plausible on a picture which takes rationality to be about having attitudes that are internally coherent.[13]

Accepting that there are no reasons for preferences is also consistent with other kinds of rational criticism of desire. Even Hume seems to grant in the above quote that desires are irrational, for example, if they are based on false beliefs. Others, such as Hubin (1991) allow rational criticism of desires which would not survive some kind of reflection or therapy. So while this picture is certainly more permissive than alternatives which accept substantive constraints, it need not be fully permissive.[14]

Second, the Humean picture of practical rationality is far from the only one which will reject *Nonarbitrariness*. A less radical view might allow that there are reasons for desires, but deny that desires are irrational whenever they're not backed up by such reasons. Lowry and Peterson (2011) argue that some grounds for desire are rationally neutral – they neither provide reasons in favor nor reasons against the desire, and having a desire on rationally neutral grounds is rationally permissible. Morality may be a helpful comparison here – moral reasons against an action can make it wrong, and moral reasons in favor of it can make it obligatory, but if there are no reasons one way or another, the action is morally permissible by default.

Third, *Nonarbitrariness* is not the only premise that is in tension with fairly common philosophical perspectives. To challenge the second premise, one would need to claim that there is a reason to prefer that experiences have a certain uncentered temporal location, which initially seems like a nonstarter. But we should not be so quick. It is certainly untenable to think that *everyone* has a reason to prefer pain on Tuesdays to pain on Mondays. But a defense against the arbitrariness argument doesn't need to claim this. It needs only to claim that *Garfield* has such a reason. One way of developing this strategy appeals to the idea that whether some fact generates a reason for an agent depends on the agent's desires. In particular, suppose we hold that one has a reason to prefer A to B if A will better satisfy one's desires than B. Then the mere fact that Garfield *does* care about temporal location could make temporal location rationally nonarbitrary for him – pain happening on Tuesday will better satisfy his desires than it happening on Monday, and therefore he has a reason for this preference. On this view, then, even if there is some requirement not to

---

[13] See Broome (2013) for a defense of a coherence view, or Kiesewetter (2020) for a reasons-responsiveness view. Żuradzki (2016) discusses the implications of these views for arguments about time bias.

[14] For a contemporary defense of a permissive picture engaging directly with uncentered time bias, see Street (2009).

be arbitrary, it can be fairly trivially satisfied, because desires can generate reasons for themselves. So defending the arbitrariness argument will require insisting that rationality demands reasons for our preferences, and *also* that our desires do not determine what counts as a reason for us in something like the way just described.

It might seem absurd, but the possibility of this kind of rational bootstrapping actually follows from some relatively familiar views – in particular, the view that we have reason to care about our self-interest paired with a *desire-satisfactionist* theory of well-being. On the simplest version of a desire-satisfactionist view, it is good for a person to have any of their desires be satisfied. The fact that Garfield *does* prefer pain on Tuesdays, on this view, makes it (in one way) better for him to experience it then. And if we have reasons to care about our self-interest, it follows that he has a reason to prefer pain on Tuesdays, and so this preference is nonarbitrary.

Desire-satisfactionists often qualify the simple version of the view in order to deal with versions of the charge that too many desires count as relevant to self-interest. It has been suggested that only desires *about one's own life* matter to one's welfare. Or only preferences which one will *knowingly* satisfy. Or only preferences which one has *while they are satisfied*. Or those which the agent *wants* to have. Or those which a *fully informed* version of the agent would want.[15] But Garfield's desires about pain are about his own life, and we can stipulate that he knows when he is satisfying them, he has them while they're satisfied, he wants to have them, and he is fully informed. So many standard adjustments to the basic desire-satisfactionist picture do not rule out Garfield's time bias affecting what is good for him.

There is something odd about these bootstrapping situations, given that Garfield's *initial* preference can't be based on the reasons which arise from that preference, and so arguably can't be rational. But we could imagine an extra step – that Garfield begins with an irrational, arbitrary preference for pain on Tuesdays. This preference makes it better for him to experience the pain then, and he might subsequently *update* the grounds for his preference to incorporate the nonarbitrary welfare consideration. This updated preference can be rational even if the original preference was not.

The main lesson here is that the success of the arbitrariness argument against even the most intuitively irrational kind of time bias requires the rejection of a family of views about the relationship between rationality, reasons, and desire which are, at least as a disjunction, quite popular. It requires the rejection of the

---

[15] See Heathwood (2016, 2019) for a discussion of some of these views and the problems they attempt to solve.

view that there are *no* reasons for desires, the view that desires on rationally neutral grounds are permissible, and at least some views that take desires to *ground* reasons, including views that take desire-satisfaction to be a component of welfare or other reason-giving source of value. The views best positioned to run the arbitrariness argument are those which both (a) take it as a requirement of rationality that our desires correspond with what is valuable, and (b) have an account of value that makes the sources of value sufficiently external to our desires.

The Argument from Prudence Against Uncentered Time Bias

The second main argument against uncentered time bias appeals to the idea that rationality involves requirements of *prudence* or self-interest.[16] An agent like Garfield, the argument goes, is irrational because they prefer what is worse for themselves. A simple version of the argument might go:

1) Rationality requires that an agent prefer outcomes that are in their overall self-interest over those that are not.
2) An agent with uncentered time bias prefers outcomes that are not in their overall self-interest over those that are.
3) So, uncentered time bias is irrational.

The first thing to observe about this argument is that it faces very similar issues to the Argument from Arbitrariness. If a roughly Humean picture on which rationality does not place substantive constraints on our basic desires is correct – whether because there are no reasons for desire at all or because such reasons always come from our desires – then rationality does not demand that we care about our self-interest. And if the right theory of well-being is a certain form of desire-satisfactionism, then as we just discussed, an agent who has an uncentered time bias might very well in virtue of that very fact be preferring outcomes that are in their own interest, threatening premise 2. So again, the success of the argument depends on rejecting these views.

But the argument from prudence has additional difficulties on top of these. Premise 1, which is an endorsement of rational *egoism*, seems too strong to be plausible – even if rationality *permits* someone to be purely self-interested, it does not intuitively *require* it. Agents who care about the well-being of others do not strike us as irrational, provided that they pursue that aim in an effective way. Weakening the claim to assert only that the agent has *some* degree of desire for their own well-being, while plausible, would break the argument. Garfield

---

[16] Brink (2011) and Sullivan (2018), for example, defend prudence-based arguments.

might care some about his overall well-being while also, independently, preferring not to undergo pain on Mondays, and therefore remain time-biased overall.

This puts the defender of an argument from prudence in an awkward position – if they are not going to commit to rational egoism, then they must provide some independent argument to the effect that an agent cannot care about the uncentered temporal location of experiences in addition to caring about their own self-interest. But such an argument – for example, the argument from arbitrariness – would if successful be sufficient on its own to rule the relevant kind of time bias out. So it will turn out that all the work is being done by this independent argument, and the idea of prudence itself plays no essential role.

The "Prudential Rationality" Strategy

Defenders of prudence-based arguments often talk of "prudential rationality," a distinctive kind of rationality that is in some way especially concerned with one's self-interest. And they sometimes put the argument from prudence in terms of this special kind of rationality. So they might instead argue:

1) Prudential rationality requires that an agent prefer outcomes that are in their overall self-interest over those that are not.
2) An agent with uncentered time bias prefers outcomes that are not in their overall self-interest over those that are.
3) So, uncentered time bias is prudentially irrational.

This is supposed to help, I think, with some of the concerns above, by maintaining an essential role for prudence in the argument while avoiding the commitment to egoism and the unwanted implication that concern with others is all-things-considered irrational. But I think it does not help much.

Putting the argument in terms of prudential rationality certainly makes it much easier, perhaps even trivial, to defend something like premise 1 – that a prudentially rational agent prefers outcomes that are in their own overall self-interest. How trivial it is depends on exactly how we characterize prudential rationality. Sullivan (2018) characterizes it as a kind of rationality that "governs what we should approve of or prefer given our self-interest" (1). Brink (2011) introduces it as a demand "that an agent act so as to promote her own overall good" (354). John Charvet (1995) builds lack of time bias into the definition directly, writing that "the idea of prudential rationality is that of a requirement of reason to treat our future interests equally as our present interests" (34). Dale Dorsey (2019), describes it as the normative domain concerned with what we owe ourselves, which is least committal about the relationship between prudential rationality and overall self-interest and so leaves most room for substantive dispute.

We do not need to adjudicate here between these different definitions. The main point to make is that while understanding prudential rationality in a narrow way may make it easier to defend a strong connection between prudential rationality and overall self-interest, this comes at a cost – the defender of this argument now has the burden of showing that there *is* such a thing as prudential rationality so understood, that it has real normative force, and that there are no other elements of rationality which compete with prudential rationality and permissibly take time into account. Otherwise, they leave open the possibility that agents like Garfield are all-things-considered rational, which will hardly be satisfying to an opponent of uncentered time bias.

Notice that even someone with a Humean, permissive picture of the rationality of desire might be perfectly willing to talk about "what we should prefer given our self-interest," as Sullivan does, if this is understood as something like "what one should prefer assuming that the only thing one desires is one's self-interest." But for the Humean this is a kind of conditional norm – caring about self-interest is purely optional from a normative perspective. We might analogously coin a special term like "competitively rational" to describe what actions or attitudes would make sense for someone given their desire to win a game. And we could even talk about "Monday-prudential rationality" to describe what would make sense for someone given a special concern with what happened to them on Monday. Garfield's bias would come out prudentially irrational but Monday-prudentially rational, and each of these claims would carry the same normative force – that is to say, none worth discussing.

The opponent of time bias using the argument from prudence, therefore, needs to say that prudential rationality is a *genuinely normative* kind of rationality, in a way competitive rationality or Monday-prudential rationality is not. And if they want to claim that there is something wrong *overall* with biased agents like Garfield, they will further need to claim that there is no other genuinely normative kind of rationality which allows caring about the uncentered temporal location of experiences, and which can outweigh or override prudential considerations when it comes to the all-things-considered rationality of our actions or attitudes.

Perhaps one can make good on this strategy by positing a very small list of genuinely normative kinds of rationality, each of which is quite particular about what preferences it allows – for example, just prudential rationality and moral rationality. Then once we find no justification for Garfield's preferences in either, we could conclude that it is in no way rational. But note that this requires making controversial claims, at least of a negative sort, not just about prudential rationality, but about what is or isn't part of rationality beyond prudence. And when prudential rationality is defined narrowly in terms of concern with one's

own well-being, such a short list seems implausible. It is plausibly permissible –
all-things-considered if not "prudentially" – for agents to have projects which
are neither targeted at their own well-being nor moral – a desire to create
beautiful art, for example. And as soon as we allow that there is some interesting
sense in which it can be rational for an agent to have and pursue those projects
despite their conflict with "prudential rationality," the door is open for someone
to claim something similar is true of preferences like Garfield's.

Another option for the "prudential rationality" strategy would involve identifying some special kind of psychological attitude, which is rationally sensitive
only to egoistic considerations. This might break the symmetry between prudential rationality and pseudo-norms like competitive rationality, which do not
govern any attitude. Then, in this limited domain, prudential concerns have no
competition, and we would not have to worry about interference from other
kinds of rationality. But then the argument could only be wielded against time
bias in this particular kind of attitude, and it does not seem like the attitudes
discussed in the context of debates over time bias, such as desire or intention,
are good candidates. Even attitudes which we'd expect for evolutionary reasons
to have a close connection with self-preservation, such as fear, do not seem
purely rationally sensitive to egoistic reasons.

Invoking a narrowly defined sense of "prudential rationality," then, does not
absolve a defender of this kind of argument of the need to defend controversial
claims about the relationship between self-interest and all-things-considered
rationality. We can conclude by stepping back and considering the relationship
between the arbitrariness and prudence arguments. If there is no rational
pressure against having arbitrary preferences, then it is hard to see how to rule
out that a rational agent might care about their own well-being in the way
prudence requires while additionally having desires like Garfield's. And if there
is rational pressure against having arbitrary preferences, then we do not need to
appeal to prudence to challenge those desires. Since the major philosophical
perspectives on rationality which pose problems for the arbitrariness argument
also pose problems for the argument from prudence, the latter looks to be in an
inferior position – committed to something more substantive about the rational
grounds of desire. Consequently, the argument from prudence does not seem to
carry significant force above that of the arbitrariness argument, at least when it
comes to uncentered time bias.

Is Uncentered Time Bias Ever Required?

So far, we have asked whether uncentered time bias is ever rationally *permissible*. But we can also ask whether any such bias is rationally *required*. There are

immediate worries about the prospects of such a claim given what we have said so far. The responses we saw to the arguments from arbitrariness and prudence involved being *flexible* about rational desire – either by insisting that there were few or no rational constraints on desires or that such desires could bootstrap themselves into rationality. And the easier it is for desires to be rational, the dimmer the possibility of rational requirements favoring time bias.

There is, to my knowledge, only one serious attempt to argue for a required uncentered time bias of any kind. In a forthcoming paper, Bradley Saad argues that it may be rationally required to have a *bias toward the earlier* – to prefer that good events happen earlier (and to prefer that bad events happen later). It is important to distinguish this unusual bias from the much more familiar *bias toward the near*, which involves preferring that good events happen *soon* – that is, earlier in the future. The latter, which we will discuss in the next section, is a centered bias, and concerns only events in the future. Bias towards the earlier applies to events in the past as well. Someone who is biased towards the earlier will be more pleased to discover that a good event happened ten thousand years ago than that it happened yesterday. They would rather a massacre have happened recently than long ago.

Saad's argument for this surprising claim is grounded in the purported plausibility of two claims, one metaphysical and one moral. First, the *growing block* theory of time, according to which the past and the present exist, but the future does not. Events become part of reality only once they happen. But after they have happened, they are part of reality forevermore. Second, a claim he calls *Amplification*: "If two (dis)valuable events differ in how long they will have (ultimately) existed but are otherwise relevantly similar, then the event that will have existed for longer will have greater (dis)value." (5). Given these two views, a good event in the distant past will ultimately be part of reality for longer than a similar one in the recent past, and therefore will have greater value. Assuming that we should prefer things that will have greater value, we should be biased towards the earlier. This is the first in a family of arguments we will see which try to justify some form of time bias on the basis of views about the metaphysics of time.

Saad's defense of *Amplification* is that "it stands to reason that more of a good thing will tend to be better and that more of a bad thing will tend to be worse." But I think it is a mistake to think that *Amplification* is supported by this platitude. It is easy to conflate an event having existed for longer with it having occurred for longer. And what is so salient about hedonic experiences in particular is that their value increases when they occur for longer. The longer that a person experiences a particular pleasure, the more of that pleasure there is, and "more of a good thing" applies. But the same is not true of the sense in which the past "exists for longer" on the growing block view. The amount of pleasure (and therefore the amount of hedonic goodness) contained in an event is fixed once it is over – it is not affected by how long that event sticks around in the museum of the past.[17]

To summarize where I would suggest things stand, we have not found any plausible case that an uncentered time bias is rationally required. And the most plausible case against uncentered time bias is the argument from arbitrariness, which is easier to defend than the argument from prudence but requires the rejection of a range of common views about how reasons are related to our desires. As they say, one man's *modus ponens* is another man's *modus tollens*, and one might draw one of two lessons. Perhaps this indicates that the case against uncentered time bias is not as strong as our intuition might suggest, given the strong theoretical commitments involved in the most powerful argument against it. Or perhaps the irrationality of uncentered time bias is so obvious that we must reject the theories which struggle to accommodate it – this is the lesson Parfit himself draws. It is for the reader to decide which direction to take, but as we will see, this choice will have serious implications for what we say about other kinds of time bias.

Part II: Near Bias

The second kind of time bias is the one most often discussed in psychology and economics – the tendency to prefer that good experiences lie in one's immediate future rather than the distant future, and the parallel tendency to prefer that bad experiences lie in the distant future rather than the immediate future. This is called *near bias* or sometimes, especially in economics, *time discounting*. This is the bias that is responsible for my disappointment upon hearing that the film I am anticipating has been delayed, and for my decision to rush to see it immediately despite the inconveniences that brings.

This tendency was criticized at least as early as Plato in the *Protagoras* (1992):

> For if someone were to say: 'But Socrates, the immediate pleasure is very much different from the pleasant and the painful at a later time,' I would reply, 'They are not different in any other way than by pleasure and pain, for there is no other

---

[17] Saad acknowledges the possibility that we might be led astray by this kind of ambiguity. He writes in response that "on the live growing block theory, events on the edge of the block and events in the block exist in the same manner. Given that longer existence at one of these locations amplifies value, we should take longer existence at the other location to do so as well." (6) But this ignores a relevant asymmetry; the duration of a hedonic event's existence on the edge of the block, because it corresponds to how long the event occurs, is relevant to how much total pleasure it will contain, but its duration of existence elsewhere in the block is not.

way that they could differ. Weighing is a good analogy; you put the pleasures together and the pains together, both the near and the remote, on the balance scale, and then say which of the two is more. (356a–b)

Socrates goes on to characterize the privileging of near pleasures to distant pleasures as a kind of misperception akin to the way objects appear larger when they are more nearby. In the *Protagoras* at least, Socrates seems to hold that it is simply impossible for someone to knowingly prefer their lesser pleasure to their greater, so for him this time bias could only be explained as a systematic mismeasurement of this kind. The economist Pigou similarly wrote that this tendency "implies only that our telescopic faculty is defective." (1920, 24–25) For our philosophical purposes, however, we will consider near bias that is not *merely* due to the belief, reasonable or not, that nearby pleasures will be greater in magnitude or more probable.

Near bias is an example of a *centered* time bias – whether an experience is in the distant or immediate future depends on when one presently is. Interestingly, although I expect near bias to strike the reader as less obviously irrational than the uncentered time bias we considered in the last section, there is a greater variety of arguments against it.

Arbitrariness and Prudence, Near Bias Edition

Versions of the arguments from Arbitrariness and Prudence we saw earlier can be marshaled against near bias as well. Reformulated, they would go:

Arbitrariness

1) *Nonarbitrariness:* At any given time, a rational agent's preferences are insensitive to arbitrary differences.
2) Whether an experience will happen soon or in the distant future is an arbitrary difference between them.
3) An agent who exhibits uncentered time bias has preferences that are sensitive to whether an experience will happen soon or in the distant future.
4) So, near bias is irrational.

Prudence

1) Rationality requires that an agent prefer outcomes that are in their self-interest over those that are not.
2) An agent with near bias prefers outcomes that are not in their self-interest over those that are.
3) So, near bias is irrational.

Parfitian Discounting

The force of these arguments against near bias is similar to their force against uncentered time bias, and many philosophers have endorsed versions of them. For example, Sidgwick (1884) writes:

> The mere difference of priority and posteriority in time is not a reasonable ground for having more regard to the consciousness of one moment than to that of another. The form in which it practically presents itself to most men is 'that a smaller present good is not to be preferred to a greater future good' (380–381).

However, there are a couple of notable complications. A number of philosophers, including Parfit (1984), McMahan (2002), and Pettigrew (2019) have claimed that rational egoistic concern, and perhaps personal identity itself, is grounded in some sort of psychological connectedness or overlap between different *time-slices* of a person – those momentary parts of them that exist at different times. Moreover, this psychological connectedness comes in degrees. Someone with Alzheimer's, for example, exhibits a lesser degree of psychological connected-ness over time than someone without it. Given this, they argue, it is rational to have *less* egoistic concern for what happens to future time-slices which are less connected to one's current self, and one is less connected to time-slices the further into the future they are. This would justify something like near bias on egoistic grounds, and perhaps identify a nonarbitrary difference between near and distant future experiences, challenging premise 2 of the arbitrariness argument and premise 1 in the argument from prudence. There is even some empirical work suggesting that perceived degrees of psychological connectedness to our future selves play an explanatory role in peoples' discounting behavior (Urminsky 2017), which might grant additional support to this idea, assuming that we should give common dispositions at least some defeasible presumption of rationality. This roughly Parfitian strategy is taken by many authors to be the best defense of something like near bias, including by some who challenge it. (Ahmed 2018)

A couple of brief points are worth making about this argument. First, on this view, the degree of rational near bias will vary significantly both between people and within a person's life – the Alzheimer's patient would rationally be more near biased than others, or than they would have been at earlier points in their life. And there are at least hypothetical agents who maintain strong psychological continu-ity throughout their lives, for whom this argument would not apply.

Second, rather than a defense of pure time bias, this attempts to ground concern for the near future in something which arguably only imperfectly correlates with proximity in time (much like uncertainty over outcomes, which we set aside earlier for precisely this reason). Depending on how we understand the relevant psychological connections, we might sometimes be more strongly connected with some of our distant future selves than our proximate selves. Suppose, for example, that I am about to undergo a severe temporary hormonal disruption which will significantly affect my personality, but that in a week the changes will be largely reverted. If these changes are significant enough, it may be that my psychological connectedness is stronger to my later selves than earlier ones, and on the view under consideration, this should manifest in something like a bias *against* the near.[18] For this sort of consideration to push unequivocally in the direction of near bias, we would need an account of the relevant psychological connections which entails that later future selves were always less strongly connected to me than earlier selves. And the stories generally provided by defenders of this kind of reasoning do not qualify.

McMahan (2002), for example, identifies one important aspect of psychological connectedness as "mental states that occur at different times but contain some internal reference to one another—for example, an experience and a later memory of that experience, or the formation of a desire or intention and the later experience of the fulfillment of that desire or intention." (74) Because we sometimes forget things only to recall them later, and because we have plenty of desires and intentions which we do not fulfill immediately, there is at best a loose relationship between temporal proximity and this kind of connectedness. Pettigrew (2019) points to shared beliefs, common values, and the connection formed when one time-slice benefits from another's sacrifice. Again, while these things may correlate with temporal proximity, they arguably do not correlate closely enough to justify an attitude deserving of the time bias label. A fresh college student who will soon go through an intellectual phase of extreme socialism before reverting to their earlier views might be justified on this view in being biased against the near.

There is also a more substantive concern about this proposal. Even supposing we grant that our distant future selves are less closely psychologically connected to us, it is not obvious *why* this should make us care less about their well-being. Why should my future time-slice having different beliefs than me, or having forgotten some of my memories, make their pleasure less important? I think this question becomes even more sharp when we recognize, as Parfit observed, that we can stand in many of these kinds of psychological relationships to other people as well. Would it be reasonable to discount other peoples' happiness on the same grounds – for instance, allowing greater suffering to occur when it is inflicted on people who do not

---

[18] More discussion of this topic can be found in Sullivan (2018, Ch. 4)

share our beliefs or values? That seems morally suspect at best, and if rational concern for ourselves is at all analogous to moral concern for others, this casts doubt on the justificatory relevance of many of the components of psychological connectedness.

I'll consider here two motivations that defenders of this strategy might appeal to in order to justify the normative significance of psychological connectedness – in each case, I suggest, even if psychological connectedness matters for *how* we should care about our future selves, the idea that we should *discount* their happiness is not well-supported.

First, one might appeal directly to intuitions. McMahan proposes a thought experiment:

The Cure

> Imagine that you are twenty years old and are diagnosed with a disease that, if untreated, invariably causes death (though not pain or disability) within five years. There is a treatment that reliably cures the disease but also, as a side effect, causes total retrograde amnesia and radical personality change. Long-term studies of others who have had the treatment show that they almost always go on to have long and happy lives, though these lives are informed by desires and values that differ profoundly from those that the person had prior to treatment. You can therefore reasonably expect that, if you take the treatment, you will live for roughly sixty more years, though the life you will have will be utterly discontinuous with your life as it has been. You will remember nothing of your past and your character and values will be radically altered. Suppose, however, that this can be reliably predicted: that the future you would have between the ages of twenty and eighty if you were to take the treatment would, by itself, be better, as a whole, than your entire life will be if you do not take the treatment. (77)

McMahan suggests that most of us would be skeptical of the rationality of taking the treatment. And, he claims, this is best explained by the welfare of the post-treatment self being discounted relative to the welfare of the untreated self in virtue of their lower psychological connectedness.

I do not have the intuition about this case that McMahan does, and I suspect that most people would take the treatment, as long as it is clear that the psychological connectedness to the post-treatment self is sufficient for survival. However, even if we grant the judgment, I think there are other explanations for a reluctance to undergo the treatment which are at least as plausible as the discount story. For a simple example, maybe some who hear the case take *being disunified* as itself a bad-making feature of a life. This could make the life which is broken into two isolated chunks overall worse even if the good things in a particular chunk are better.

Or, to take an explanation I find even more plausible, consider the following principle:

Present-Aim Privilege: It is rational for an agent at time **t** to favor the realization of goals they have at **t** over goals they do not have at **t**.

Parfit (1984) argues for a stronger version of this according to which one rationally tries to satisfy *only* one's present desires, but even the weaker version here is sufficient to explain why someone might have second thoughts about taking the cure. Someone in that position will have various goals that will be realized better by not taking the treatment – they likely have projects important to them that they will be able to complete with five more years, and they care a lot about being able to spend even a little remaining time with their loved ones while retaining their memories of them. Of course, if they took the treatment, they would complete other projects and spend time with other loved ones, but those aren't goals they have right now, so according to *Present-Aim Privilege*, their realization is less rationally important to the agent (and perhaps rationally irrelevant). One of their present goals, no doubt, is to live a long and happy life, and this particular goal would be satisfied better by the treatment, but nothing guarantees this consideration will outweigh the others.

It's important to see that although privileging present aims may look superficially like discounting future selves which are less closely psychologically connected, these are very distinct explanations. The Present-Aim view tells you not to care so much about realizing the projects of future selves when you do not share those projects, but this is not the same as *discounting the value of their pleasure*. If I care now about living a pleasant life, then the view will not tell me to discount the pleasure of future selves no matter how dissimilar we are.

There is of course considerable controversy over whether *Present-Aim Privilege* is correct.[19] But it does not need to be correct in order for it to provide an alternative explanation of people's reactions to cases like *The Cure*, as long as people are implicitly sympathetic to it. With multiple candidate explanations for the intuitions in that case, we should look for other test cases. And there are cases that I believe tell strongly against the Parfitian discounting story.

The Hyde Pill

Jekyll has a serious illness which will kill him unless he undergoes a special form of treatment, which has two parts, and which is scheduled a week from now. One part requires him to take a pill which will, over a short period, gradually put him into a state where he will not remember his past life, and during which his personality

---

[19] Kagan (1986) contains a critical discussion of Parfit's arguments.

will be significantly altered. This state will last for a day and then he will gradually regain his other memories and personality. Another part requires him to undergo a very painful operation, during which he must remain conscious. However, he can choose the order of the two parts. He can have the operation a day before taking the pill, or while he is under its effects. However, due to certain physiological side effects of the pill, if he has the operation while under its effects, the operation will last two hours, when otherwise it would last only one.

Should Jekyll choose to undergo the operation before or after taking the pill? I think it is fairly clear that he should choose the less-painful operation. But if the Parfitian discounting story is correct, it seems like Jekyll has just as much reason to choose the more painful operation as you have to resist the treatment in *The Cure*, since Jekyll today is only weakly psychologically connected to Jekyll under the Hyde pill's effects. If the discounting power of connectedness is significant enough to justify trading forty good but weakly connected years for five strongly connected ones, then it should certainly be significant enough to justify trading one strongly connected hour of suffering for two weakly connected hours. If I am right about this case, then even those who agree with McMahan about *The Cure* should reject the Parfitian discounting explanation of the case.

Alienation

A different way of justifying this form of discounting, suggested by Pettigrew (2019), draws an analogy between the view that one rationally ought to be neutral with respect to time and utilitarianism, the view that one ought morally to maximize the welfare of everyone impartially. Temporal neutrality, Pettigrew argues, is an intrapersonal analog of interpersonal impartiality, and so it's not surprising it will face similar worries. There is an objection to utilitarianism, notably pressed by Peter Railton (1984), which accuses the view of *alienating* the moral agent in an objectionable way by requiring her to treat her own projects, concerns, and relationships as subservient to the general impersonal good. In Railton's words, this makes utilitarianism's recommendations "an alien set of demands, distant and disconnected from [my] actual concerns" (135). Pettigrew suggests that just as the utilitarian agent is alienated by the requirement to be impartial towards all other people, the temporally neutral agent's present self is alienated by the requirement to give equal weight to the interests of future versions of herself which do not share many of her beliefs, traits, or values.

However, there are several obstacles to this strategy. First, it is controversial whether alienation generates a successful objection even against utilitarianism.[20] Second, it is not clear whether the kind of alienation involved in the intrapersonal

---

[20] See Baker and Maguire (2020) for a discussion of several strategies in the literature.

case is problematic in the same way as the kind facing utilitarianism. Discussion of alienation in the literature tends to focus around the utilitarian agent's impersonal perspective towards their relationships with others and how it renders the agent incapable of realizing morally important values like genuine friendship. It is not obvious that there are similarly significant values which are lost to the agent who is temporally neutral.

But even putting these concerns to one side, I think there is a further problem – discounting by things like degree of psychological overlap is not the right way to respond to the threat of alienation. Taking the analogy between the intrapersonal and interpersonal case seriously, discounting the welfare of future selves who do not share your values, beliefs, traits, and memories is like modifying utilitarianism to grant more weight to the welfare of people who are similar to you. And besides being an obvious nonstarter as a moral view, this would not remove the worry about alienation. What is alienating about the demands of utilitarianism is not that the people whose interests swamp your special connection to your personal projects are different or distant from you – it would be just as alienating to be forced to shelve those projects for the well-being of people like you. To address alienation, a view needs to allow me to treat *my* projects as special. This suggests, by analogy, that alienation in the intrapersonal case isn't resolved by discounting, but by treating my *present* projects as special – that is, by something like *Present-Aim Privilege*.

I will make one final point about alienation. My future selves will be connected to me in some respects, and disconnected from me in others. Perhaps my future self maintains my love for philosophy, has lost my love for movies, and has gained a love for competitive underwater hockey. I can imagine there being something alienating about being required now to respect my future self's concern for winning underwater hockey games, which strikes me now as bizarre and pointless. But there doesn't seem to be anything alienating about being required to respect their philosophical ambitions, which I share and understand. The point here is that how alienating it is to respect some future self's concern is a function of my psychological relationship to *that concern*, not my overall psychological connectedness to the self which has it. But the views defended by Parfit, McMahan, and Pettigrew tell us there is a *general* discount rate for the interests of each future self. So these views do not seem like the best way to develop a discounting view motivated by alienation.

I think there is some value in developing a more sophisticated psychological discounting view which is more granular in its treatment of various future interests. But I do not think such a view will be of much help when it comes to justifying something like the time-discounting of hedonic goods which is our primary concern. My underwater hockey phase comes and goes, and many details of what I want out of my life change as I get older – the importance of family, or career, or legacy. But throughout all of it, I at least want my life to be pleasant and not painful. Our concern with pleasure and pain is perhaps the least likely of all of our desires to be disrupted by time, and so a view that discounts at the level of individual concerns by our identification with or connection to that concern is unlikely to justify an overall hedonic bias towards the near.

Partiality and Bonds of Concern

A different though related strategy for defending the rationality of near bias is proposed by Dale Dorsey (2019). Dorsey's argument exploits an analogy with the ethics of partial concern. Moral commonsense seems to acknowledge a prerogative to grant additional weight to the concerns of people with whom we have special relationships, such as our family members or partners. If this is true of morality, Dorsey suggests, then it is plausible that there is also a *rational* prerogative to grant additional weight to the concerns of time-slices of me which are related to me in similar special ways. And, he claims, it is plausible that at least for most of us, nearer time-slices are more closely related to us in those special ways than further time-slices.

The success of this strategy depends on whether the grounds for partiality to others – what Dorsey calls the *bonds of concern*, are replicated between time-slices of the same individual. However, I do not think the prospects of this are good. Many common justifications for special consideration of close relationships simply will not do the job Dorsey needs. For example, partial concern for our parents is sometimes explained as repayment of debt, or as an expression of gratitude, for them raising us or bringing us into existence. But my concern for future time-slices cannot be justified by what they have done for me. Special concern for our friends or partners is sometimes explained as an appropriate response to the experiences we have shared, or implicit promises we have made through interacting with each other in certain ways. But there are no experiences I have shared with my near future time-slices which I have not also shared with my distant future time-slices, and no obvious implicit promises I have made to them. Keller (2006) suggests that partial concern can be justified because there are *special goods* that can only be provided by those who stand in certain relationships with us. Again, it is hard to see what special goods I can provide to my near future self which I could not provide to my distant future self, and in any case, near bias covers the provision of very unspecial goods like pleasure.

Dorsey may not be moved by these worries because even if all these other grounds for partial concern do not apply, "it is at least *quite plausible* to hold that the fact that I deeply care for some person, indeed, care for this person more than others, can itself be a moral reason that justifies granting their interests greater weight." (463), and the facts about our near bias show we care for our near future time-slices in the right way.

But there is a problem with this reasoning which takes the form of a dilemma. On the one hand, if "caring for someone" is read in a thin way, such that granting someone's interest greater weight is *itself* sufficient for caring, then it is not plausible that mere caring provides a moral reason to favor someone's interest. This would make favoring someone's interest trivially self-justifying in a way that intuitively it is not – the mere fact that someone *does* favor the interests of some arbitrary group – green-eyed people, for example – does not by itself justify their doing so. If, on the other hand, "caring for someone" is read in a thicker way, such that it involves attitudes like *love*, then it is more plausible that caring is sufficient for partiality, but less obvious that I do care about my near future self in the right way.[21] In any case, the mere fact of near time bias is not good evidence that I do.

If I am right that these arguments have serious deficiencies, then the case from arbitrariness and prudence is about as strong against near bias as it is against uncentered time bias.

Near Bias and Action Over Time

Perhaps the biggest difference between the dialectic over uncentered time bias and near bias is the emergence of a new kind of argument which purports to show certain time preferences irrational via their implications for the behavior of the agent across time. Near bias of certain kinds, it is argued, renders the agent *exploitable* in ways that rationality prohibits.

To sketch how this works, let us consider how a near-biased agent might value a given quantity of pleasure, to be received at different times. Let us stipulate Subira values pleasure fully when it is immediate, and then discounts it very sharply, asymptotically approaching a minimum of 1/5th its full value, such that the following is a graph of the value Subira will place on the prospect of ten units of pleasure which are currently two months away, and five units of pleasure which are currently one month away (Figure 1).

The crucial thing to observe about this graph is the moment, shortly before the one-month mark, where these two lines cross. Before this point, Subira prefers the distant ten units. After this point, she prefers the nearby five units. This means if we approached Subira right now, she should be willing to pay

---

21 An example account of a robust form of self-love can be found in Bransen (2015), though notably his conception of self-love does not involve disproportionate concern with one's own welfare, so it would not easily be conscripted to justify the kind of time bias we are investigating.

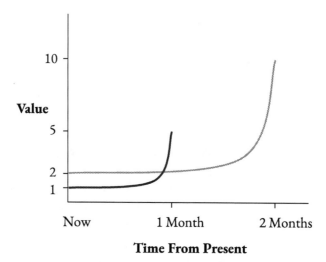

Figure 1 Hyperbolic discounting of value – five units one month
away (dark) and ten units two months away (light).

some cost in order to trade a nearby five units of pleasure for a distant ten. And
then if we approach her again immediately before the month arrives, after the
lines have crossed, she should be willing to pay some cost in order to trade ten
units in a month for an immediate five units, effectively reversing the effect of
the first trade. By paying a cost twice in order to end up otherwise in the same
position as if she had accepted neither offer, Subira has been *money pumped* or
exploited. And this, the argument goes, shows she is irrational. Similar exploitation arguments are familiar in epistemology in the form of *dutch book* arguments for having credences that satisfy the probability axioms, or for updating
beliefs on the basis of the *conditionalization* rule, making this strategy particularly appealing to those who accept those arguments.[22]

   The graph we drew above only represents one way an agent might be near-
biased. But several proofs have been given since Strotz (1955) to the effect that
there is only one kind of systematic discounting which will not lead to this kind
of exploitation – *exponential discounting*. Someone discounts exponentially
when they have a *constant discount rate* – if they discount the value of pleasure
by a certain proportion between two particular times, they discount pleasure by
that rate between *any* two times separated by the same interval. The graph of the
value of two prospective goods at different times for an exponential discounter
will have lines that never cross, and so they are not exploitable in the same way.

---

[22]   For other Elements in this series which discuss these kinds of arguments in depth, see Pettigrew
(2020) and Gustafsson (2022).

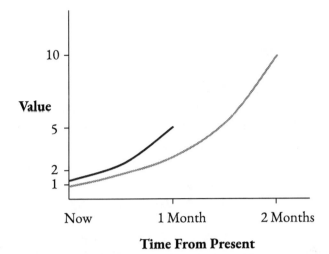

Time From Present

Figure 2 Exponential discounting of value – five units one month away (dark) and ten units two months away (light).

In situations of deferred pleasures like Subira's, a graph of their preferences will look something like this (Figure 2).

Many economists and philosophers conclude that there is something irrational about all forms of near bias that are not exponential discounting. A first-pass sketch of the argument (which will require significant revision, as we will see) would go as follows:

1) If a near-biased agent does not discount exponentially, they are exploitable.
2) If an agent is exploitable, they are irrational.
3) So, if a near-biased agent does not discount exponentially, they are irrational.

There are several points worth noting about the relationship between this kind of argument to earlier arguments we have discussed. First, agents with consistent, purely *uncentered* time biases, like Garfield, are not exploitable in this way – their value for the prospect of a given amount of pleasure on a given day is unaffected by which day it currently is.

Second, this kind of argument might be successful even on the Humean views which do not place substantive constraints on what kinds of things a rational agent might desire, and which we saw were grounds for rejecting other arguments against time bias. Being subject to exploitation, it is often thought, reveals a *structural* defect in one's attitudes, and structural requirements are accepted even by those who deny key premises in the prudence and arbitrariness arguments, such as the rational necessity of egoistic concern or the prohibition against arbitrary preferences.

Third, although this argument technically leaves exponential discounting untouched, it might play a dialectical role in rejecting the rationality of near bias altogether. If, for example, the best defense of near bias relies on either the psychological connectedness or the partiality justifications we discussed in the previous section, then it will be undermined if it can be shown that the kind of near bias these justifications suggest is not exponential discounting.

Arif Ahmed (2018) gives precisely this sort of argument against discounting in virtue of psychological connectedness. Ahmed's reasoning that this sort of discounting is not exponential involves making certain simplifying assumptions about how the number of psychological connections is related to the appropriate discount rate, modeling an agent with multiple psychological connections that are eroding at different rates, and showing that their appropriate discount rate is not constant. However, I think this mathematical approach is unnecessarily complicated. As we noted in the previous section, it is not even clear that psychological connectedness strictly diminishes, and there is no reason whatso-ever to think that it does so at a rate systematic enough to justify exponential discounting. Indeed, the existence of conditions which speed the rate of decay is enough to rule this out. If there are two agents who have psychological connections decaying in a similar way, and one of them acquires Alzheimer's, then their justified discount rates will be different going forward, and so it cannot be that both maintain the constant rate required for exponential discount-ing. A similar lesson would apply to Dorsey's bonds of concern. There is no reason to expect the strength of bonds of concern between time-slices to be systematically related in the way necessary for this justification to imply exponential discounting.

Another way this debate might bear on the broader question of near bias concerns our actual discounting dispositions. One potential reason to favor the rationality of near bias is simply that actual human beings clearly regularly exhibit it, and one might reasonably grant some defeasible presumption in favor of the rationality of near-universal dispositions. However, evidence suggests that actual human discounting is not exponential, and is better approximated by a *hyperbolic* discount function, according to which the discount rate diminishes as prospects go further into the future, rather than remaining constant.[23] Hyperbolic discounters are exploitable, so if the argument is correct, this plausibly undermines the defeasible support our actual discounting practice might provide to the rationality of near bias.

---

[23] Ainslie & Halsam (1992) represent early work arguing for this claim. Wang et al. (2016) get similar results across a wider range of countries.

The success of the exploitation argument, then, matters not just for narrowing down which *types* of near bias are rationally acceptable, but also for the greater debate about whether any near bias can be justified at all. However, the exploitation argument faces serious challenges.

Stationarity

The first problem is that premise 1 is not quite true. Diachronic exploitability cannot be shown merely from the way an agent values prospects at a single time – we must assume something about how they value those prospects at all of the times they are offered the relevant decisions. In particular, the arguments showing exploitability (or unexploitability) assume near-biased agents are biased *in the same way* at these different times, in the following sense: If I now discount the value of goods that are some delay Δ into the future by some factor (relative to the same good now), then tomorrow, I will discount goods that are then Δ in the future by the same factor. Or in other words, my preferences at a time *t* between the prospect of fixed goods at other times depend only on when those times are relative to *t*. I follow Ahmed (2018) and Pettigrew (2019) in calling this *Stationarity*, although there seems to be some inconsistency in the literature; Halevy (2015) and Callender (2023), for example, call this "*Time Invariance*" and use "*Stationarity*" for a different principle.

To see the role *Stationarity* plays, suppose it's Monday, and an agent applies a 50 percent discount to pleasure tomorrow rather than today, but only a 33 percent discount to pleasure in two days rather than tomorrow. If they were stationary, and discounted the same way on Tuesday as on Monday, they would be exploitable. Right now we could offer to give them ten units of pleasure on Wednesday in exchange for six units on Tuesday and a small fee, and they would accept, because a 33 percent discount on ten units is still greater than six. Then, tomorrow, we could offer to undo the trade for another small fee, and they would accept, because a 50 percent discount on ten units is less than six.

But if they violate *Stationarity*, it is possible for them to avoid being exploited. In particular, they could become *more patient* on Tuesday, so that instead of applying a 50 percent discount to tomorrow's pleasure, they only apply a 33 percent discount. This means on Tuesday, they discount Wednesday's pleasure relative to Tuesday's by the same rate they did on Monday (in fact, their preferences resemble those of someone who simply has a consistent uncentered time bias favoring earlier times). And this means they will not flip their preferences and accept a loss to undo their earlier decision.

This means that to get the exploitation argument off the ground, we need to find some way to incorporate *Stationarity*. There are a few ways to do this. First, one might use it to limit the argument's conclusion, so that it proves only that non-exponential discounting is irrational for agents who *do* happen to satisfy *Stationarity*, while allowing that there may be rational agents who violate it:

1) If a near-biased agent satisfies *Stationarity* and does not discount exponentially, they are exploitable.
2) If an agent is exploitable, then they are irrational.
3) So, a near-biased agent who satisfies *Stationarity* and does not discount exponentially is irrational.

However, this version of the argument is not likely to satisfy those looking to leverage exploitation against near bias in general or those looking to defend exponential discounting. If you were opposed to near bias, or certain kinds of near bias, you probably thought it was irrational for me to discount my future well-being in the relevant way *right now*, and not just irrational for me to combine discounting it that way right now and discounting it in certain ways in the future. It doesn't seem like the appropriateness of an agent's discounting the future in some way should depend on what happens *later*.

So dialectically it makes sense to try and preserve a stronger conclusion that does not require us to wait and see what an agent does later before criticizing their near bias. The most straightforward, and the strategy taken in the literature, is to insist that *Stationarity* is itself a requirement of rationality. The argument would then run:

1) If a near-biased agent satisfies *Stationarity* and does not discount exponentially, they are exploitable.
2) If an agent is exploitable, then they are irrational.
3) If an agent does not satisfy *Stationarity*, they are irrational.
4) So, a near-biased agent who does not discount exponentially is irrational.

If these premises are all correct we do not have to wait and see what happens to the agent before convicting them of irrationality, because no matter how their preferences evolve, they will violate at least one rational requirement – either the prohibition on exploitation or the requirement to satisfy *Stationarity*. In exchange, though, the new premise 3 must be defended. What can be said in favor of it? Ahmed (2018) insists that rejecting premise 3 would be unsatisfactory because "it makes [the agent's] present evaluation of a future delay depend not only on the futurity and length of that delay but also on what date it is now. More specifically, her rate of time-preference at any time is a function of the date t—typically a declining function, so that the longer she lives the more patient she gets. But why should her past longevity have normative bearing on her present concern for her future self?" (253)

But it is difficult to see the force of Ahmed's reasoning here. Someone who rejects *Stationarity* as a rational requirement does not, as Ahmed implies, have to hold that past longevity has normative bearing on present concern. First of all, they need not make any positive claims about normative bearing at all. They need not claim that satisfying *Stationarity* is rationally *prohibited*, only permissible. And some pattern of preferences might be permissible even if there is no positive normative reason favoring it over other equally permissible patterns.

Moreover, even someone who does think that certain agents are required to violate *Stationarity* needn't think that the explanation is that "past longevity" or the date is *itself* normatively significant. As Pettigrew (2019) points out, someone who discounts on the basis of psychological connectedness and knows they are more closely psychologically connected between Monday and Tuesday than between Friday and Saturday will discount tomorrow less when it is Monday than when it is Friday, violating *Stationarity* but not treating time itself as having any normative significance.

It is hard to find other arguments in favor of *Stationarity* as a rational requirement which do not beg the question. In the economics literature, it is sometimes taken as axiomatic. Callender (2023), though ultimately unsympathetic to the attempt to use Stationarity to argue for exponential discounting, suggests that the best way to make it plausible appeals to temporal neutrality itself. However, this would be clearly dialectically inappropriate in a context like ours where temporal neutrality is precisely what is up for debate.

At the same time, there are several arguments against *Stationarity*'s candidacy as a rational requirement. A number of philosophers have recently argued for some version of what is called *time-slice rationality* – the thesis that all rational norms are *synchronic*. On the time-slice view, rational norms apply to individual time-slices of agents and are satisfied or violated only in virtue of those time-slices in isolation. *Stationarity* would be a diachronic requirement – someone violates it only in virtue of what they are like over an extended period of time. Anyone who endorses such a requirement, then, must contend with the arguments of the time-slicers.

Hedden (2015a) argues for the time-slice picture on two grounds. First, it is common to hold that norms of rationality are *internalist* – your rationality supervenes on "your perspective" – that is, your mental states. If something is rational for one agent, then it is rational for their psychological twin, who has the same beliefs, desires, and other mental states, even if facts outside their awareness are different. Taking this seriously, Hedden thinks, should also lead you to endorse that the perspective relevant for your current rationality is your *current* perspective. The mental states of past or future time-slices of you, while you might *care* about them in a special way, are outside of the perspective relevant for evaluating your rationality in just the way the mental states of other people are outside of your perspective.

Second, if what is rational for an agent can depend on features of their past and future time-slices, then in order to assess an agent's rationality, we will have to know which past and future time-slices are time-slices of *them*. This means that rationality will depend on facts about *personal identity* over time. And there are a number of infamous thought experiments, many discussed by Parfit (1984), where it is quite controversial whether someone at one time is the same person as someone at another time. For example, if I step into a machine which, when activated, scans my body, destroys it, and then simultaneously uses the results of the scan to create a duplicate of that body in a different location, is the resulting person me? That is, have I been transported, or have I been destroyed? If a diachronic norm, like *Stationarity*, is a rational requirement, then the answer to this question matters for rationality. If the pre-activation agent discounts in one way, and the post-activation agent discounts in a different way, then whether there is a violation of *Stationarity* depends on whether those are the same agent. Hedden's argument is that while it is unclear what to say about personal identity in such cases, we do not need to settle that kind of question in order to tell whether the pre-activation and post-activation agent is behaving rationally. While the arguments for time-slice rationality are by no means widely accepted,[24] it is a cost to this kind of argument if it must take a stand on this kind of controversy.

A different reason to be skeptical about *Stationarity* notes that preferences about when good things occur relative to the present are just one kind of preference among many. But most people and philosophers alike do not take preference change in general to be irrational. Perhaps when I am young it is important to me that I will have a successful career, but once I have a child the well-being of my family becomes much more important. The literature on so-called *transformative experiences* (much inspired by Paul 2014) discusses particularly stark examples of this kind, and while there are many disagreements about how a rational agent might make decisions when these experiences are in the offing, it is widely thought that simply undergoing these experiences is not irrational. So someone who takes *Stationarity* as a rational requirement must either adopt a counterintuitive stance on the rationality of preference change in general, or show some relevant distinction between time preferences and other sorts of preferences which explains why the former, but not the latter, must hold constant.

---

[24] See Podgorski (2016) for several challenges to Hedden's picture.

To make things more difficult, a natural way to argue that other kinds of preference change are irrational is by showing that an agent who changes their preference is exploitable. If I prefer apples to oranges on Monday, and oranges to apples on Tuesday, then I will trade an orange at some cost for an apple on Monday, and then trade back the next day, being worse-off for no gain. This is true of temporally uncentered preferences, whether they concern uncentered temporal location or nontemporal phenomena. But as we have seen, when it comes to centered temporal preferences, change might be the only thing *preventing* the agent from being exploitable.

There is a final way to fit *Stationarity* into the argument which has not been explored in the literature but which I think has much to recommend it over the previous options. For reasons that should become clear, I will set it aside until we discuss another major point of contention in the exploitability argument.

Exploitation and Irrationality

The formulations of the exploitation argument we have looked at have a further worry. Why should we think that being exploitable is irrational?

An initially tempting answer is that the problem with being exploitable is that an exploited agent (for instance Subira in our example) ends up predictably *overall worse-off* than if they had some pattern of preferences that didn't lead to exploitation, and that rationality prohibits patterns of desire that predictably make one worse-off. But I think this would be the wrong way to interpret the issue. We don't need anything as fancy as the exploitation argument to show us that a near-biased agent, *whether or not* they discount exponentially, ends up making themselves overall worse-off than someone without a time preference. That is clear just from looking at a single decision, where the agent sacrifices greater pleasure later for less pleasure now. If we are accepting a strong connection between rationality and overall self-interest, then we might as well just run the argument from prudence, which does not require us to defend the rationality of *Stationarity* and which is more powerful, giving us grounds to reject non-exponential discounting, exponential discounting, and uncentered time biases all in one fell swoop.

If there is a special kind of problem with exploitability, which moves the debate over time bias forward, then, it is not that it is bad from the point of view of the agent's overall welfare taken impartially, but that it is bad from each of the agent's biased points of view as well. The situation where Subira rejects both offers is not only better for Subira overall than the one where she takes both – it is preferable even from her earlier and later time-biased perspectives, since the distribution of goods is the same except for the pure cost of buying the offers.

She is sometimes better-off and never worse-off if she takes neither offer, so this is preferable no matter which time-slice we ask, and no matter how much each time-slice discounts the future, as long as they give it any weight at all.

But even this is not obviously rationality impugning, for several reasons. First, the rational requirement not to be exploitable is subject to some of the same worries that faced *Stationarity* in the previous section. Because an agent like Subira is exploitable only in virtue of decisions she makes across different times, accepting that exploitation is rationally objectionable requires a diachronic conception of rational norms and therefore again requires us to reject *time-slice rationality*. And if exploitability is in general irrational, then it seems changes in nontemporal preferences must be irrational. As we saw, an agent who prefers apples on Monday and oranges on Tuesday will accept trades making themselves strictly poorer than if they had done nothing at all. But at least some kinds of preference change – those involved in transformative experiences, if not mundane instances involving fruit – do *not* strike most of us as irrational. So once again, the defender of this argument must take a counterintuitive stand on the rationality of preference change.

Pettigrew (2019, 2020) also argues that exploitable preferences are not always irrational. Exploitation is problematic, Pettigrew suggests, when it indicates that there is some alternative for the agent that would be better for the agent from any of their actual future and past perspectives and no matter how things turn out. However, although in Subira's case, there is an alternative pair of *decisions* (accepting neither offer) which is better than the decisions she ends up making, from all her perspectives, it does not follow that there are any alternative *preferences* she might have which would outperform her exploitable time-biased preferences in the relevant way. For any other preference profile she might have had, there will be some decision situations in which those preferences would lead to a worse decision than her actual exploitable preferences would, from the perspective of at least some of her actual preferences. For example, if she had no time bias at all, then she would avoid exploitation, but she would (among other things) refuse an immediate five units of pleasure in exchange for ten in a month, when that is the only offer that is ever presented to her. And that is not preferable from her actual present perspective. So her exploitable preferences are not strictly inferior to the unbiased preferences in the way necessary to convict them of irrationality, even though in *some* worlds they lead her to make strictly inferior choices.

Another objection, raised in some form by Levi (2002) and Hedden (2015b) suggests that exploitability is only a sign of irrationality when one has at some time control over all of the actions in virtue of which one is exploited. But while Subira has at one time control over whether she accepts the first offer, and at a different time control over whether she accepts the second offer, she does not at any point have control over both offers. If she had control over both offers, then she would decide to buy the first offer and then reject the second, and she would avoid exploitation. This suggests that the kind of diachronic exploitability at work in this argument (and certain other exploitation arguments, for instance in favor of Bayesian conditionalization) is rationally unproblematic.

The Kantian Exploitability Argument

As we have seen, both the role of *Stationarity* and the appeal to the irrationality of diachronic exploitation raise serious worries about the exploitation argument as it has generally been understood. However, I'd like to sketch an alternative strategy that has been underexplored but which I think has much to recommend it over the previous options. Consider this variant of the exploitation argument:

1) If a near-biased agent satisfies *Stationarity* and does not discount exponentially, they are exploitable.
2) If an agent *would be* exploitable if they satisfied *Stationarity*, then they are irrational.
3) So, a near-biased agent that does not discount exponentially is irrational.

The new premise 2 in this argument replaces the work done by the earlier argument's commitment to the irrationality of violating *Stationarity* and the irrationality of exploitability. But this modification will no doubt strike the reader as strange. Why would an agent be irrational just because they *would* be exploitable under some additional, perhaps non-actual condition, unless that condition was itself rationally required, and unless exploitability was itself rationally defective?

But I think this maneuver is not as wild as it might seem. The motivating idea is that having a certain discounting attitude towards the future rationally commits you to something – not to *actually later having* the same attitude – that would take us back to thinking *Stationarity* is a rational requirement – but to in some sense *currently endorsing* having that attitude in the future. And though there might be nothing wrong with being exploitable as such, there is something wrong with endorsing at a single time a pattern of attitudes that renders you exploitable.[25]

This argument has something of a Kantian character. On Kant's moral view, acting according to a given principle commits you to endorsing it as a principle

---

[25] Dougherty (2011) makes a similar appeal to rational endorsement in the context of an argument against future bias discussed in the next section. This strategy has some resemblance to the approach taken by Christensen (1996) in his reinterpretation of exploitation arguments in epistemology.

for all other rational beings. And if there would be something self-defeating about your action when all other rational beings act on the same principle, then you cannot rationally or morally act on that principle.[26] Our argument is structurally similar, except that we are speaking of preferences rather than principles of action, and the commitment is more narrow – having a preference doesn't commit you to endorsing *everyone* having that preference, but commits you to endorsing *your* having that preference in the future.

Bringing out this Kantian reasoning, a more complete argument might look something like this:

1) If a near-biased agent satisfies *Stationarity* and does not discount exponentially, they are exploitable.
2) A near-biased agent is rationally committed to endorsing the preferences they would have if they satisfied *Stationarity*.
3) It is irrational to endorse preferences which render you exploitable.
4) So, If an agent *would be* exploitable if they satisfied *Stationarity*, then they are irrational. (From 2, 3)
5) So, a near-biased agent that does not discount exponentially is irrational.

One important feature of this argument that distinguishes it from the earlier exploitation arguments is that it appeals only to *synchronic* constraints of rationality. If an agent discounts in a non-exponential way, right now, they are irrational in virtue of their current attitudes of endorsement, and not because they will later inevitably violate some requirement. Consequently, this argument is able to both do justice to the idea that we do not need to wait and see before criticizing a time-biased agent, and remain consistent with the purely synchronic time-slice picture of rationality.

It also promises to avoid the worry about the earlier arguments that the reasoning overgeneralizes to imply, counterintuitively, that all preference change is irrational. Take an agent who undergoes a preference change, for example, who ages out of valuing career success into valuing close relationships. Although this change in preferences means they can be exploited over time, at no point do they *endorse* all the preferences which lead to their exploitation. When they are young and career-focused, they may view their future preferences as an unfortunate if perhaps inevitable going-soft. And when they are older and relationship-focused, they may view their earlier preferences as the misguided priorities of the inexperienced. But if an agent is near-biased, the thought goes, they cannot view the preferences they end up with by

---

[26] For discussions of different interpretations of this part of Kant's view, see Korsgaard (1985)

satisfying *Stationarity* as misguided in the same way, for those preferences reflect the very same attitude towards the future they currently have – to dismiss them as folly would in some sense be incoherent.

Although I think something like this Kantian strategy is probably the best way to develop the exploitation worry, it is not without its worries. In particular, more must be said about the nature of the "endorsement" which the argument targets for rational assessment. Endorsement of a preference cannot, for example, be the belief that the preference is rational, because that would make premise 3 assert that it is irrational to believe that it is rational to have exploitable preferences, and committing to this would undermine the supposed advantage this argument has of remaining neutral on the rationality of exploitability as such. Moreover, it simply does not seem irrational for every agent to believe in the rationality of exploitable preferences, even if that belief is in fact false. Beliefs are rationally subject to the evidence, and we can imagine someone having good evidence for the rationality of exploitability (for instance, testimony by thoughtful experts like Pettigrew) even if the view is incorrect.[27]

Endorsement of a preference also arguably should not be understood as a *desire* to have that preference, because it is hard to see why a rational agent must desire to have future preferences which are stationary relative to their current preferences, and therefore why premise 2 would be plausible under this interpretation. Indeed, if an agent has some kind of near bias, then it seems like the discounting it is rational for them to desire to have between two future times should match their *current* relative discount between those future times, rather than the discount they would have, if they satisfied *Stationarity*, once those times arrived. For example, if I currently care more about pleasure today than pleasure tomorrow, but am totally indifferent between pleasure tomorrow and pleasure at all later times, then I should, right now, desire to be temporally neutral in a year – that will make me most likely to act then in a way that gives me the distribution of pleasure that matches my current values.

The success of the Kantian argument, then, depends on identifying a species of endorsement, which makes the premises of the argument plausible without undermining the advantages it has over the other arguments we've discussed. Given that the most natural candidates for identifying endorsement with belief and identifying endorsement with desires do not seem to work, there is some work for a defender of this argument to do before we can call it an improvement. Nevertheless, I think the value of being able to avoid worries about diachronic rationality in general and about diachronic exploitability in particular is

---

[27] Some philosophers deny this – for example, if they accept a strong version of the thesis that "mistakes about rationality are mistakes of rationality" (Titelbaum 2015). But even Titelbaum, who defends this view, takes it to be a counterintuitive position.

considerable, and this issue warrants a deeper exploration than it has been given in the literature.

Part III: Future Bias

Once we have factored out uncertainty and other things that are correlated with how distant events would be in the future, accepting that near bias is irrational might seem quite natural. But one of the things that makes the topic of time bias so interesting and so puzzling is that there is another bias, subject to similar philosophical criticism, which is much harder to dismiss. This is *future bias* – the preference for pleasures to be in the future rather than the past, and a corresponding preference for pains being in the past rather than the future. When I walk out of the theater and regret that I now have an experience to look back on rather than forward to, and am jealous of my friends who have yet to watch the movie for the first time, it is future bias at work. Like near bias, this is a *centered* time bias – whether a pleasure is past or future depends on when *now* is.[28]

Parfit (1984) discusses a case like the following, which brings out the intuitive pull of future bias:

Past or Future Operation

> Dolores is at the hospital for treatment. Based on the results of her tests, the doctors either assigned her the Early Operation or the Late Operation, both of which must be undergone without anesthetic. The Early Operation will happen on Monday, will take two painful hours, and will induce a temporary amnesia, so the next day she will not remember whether she has undergone it. The Late Operation will happen on Wednesday and will take just one (equally) painful hour. Dolores wakes up, sees on the calendar that it is Tuesday, and is not sure which operation was scheduled for her. She asks the doctor whether she already had the longer operation, or whether she is soon to have the shorter one.

Which answer is it reasonable for Dolores to hope for from the doctor? Which answer should she be relieved to hear? Parfit expects most to maintain that Dolores should hope that her operation is in the past, even though if it is in the past, it is twice as painful. Indeed, there is some temptation to say that she should prefer the operation be in the past even if it was ten or a hundred times more painful. Some philosophers, such as Heathwood (2008) suggest that it is reasonable to prefer *any* amount of pain in the past to even the slightest pain in the future. For simplicity, for the rest of our discussion, I will be treating future

---

[28] There is much less empirical work investigating actual humans' future bias than near bias. Caruso et al. (2008) is a rare example.

bias as absolute in this way, but versions of all the arguments we will discuss apply to non-absolute future bias as well.

Notably, at least as far as my intuition goes, Dolores does not merely seem *permitted* to prefer that her pain is in the past – a reaction of "thank goodness" or a shrug of indifference when her doctor informs her that the operation is still ahead of her would be quite bizarre. So common sense arguably treats future bias as rationally required.

Defenders of time neutrality are well aware of the force of the future bias intuition. But, they typically argue, arguments analogous to those against other intuitively irrational forms of time bias generalize to future bias as well, so these biases ultimately fall together.

Arbitrariness and Prudence, Future Bias Edition

It should come as little surprise that our old friends Prudence and Arbitrariness find their way back into this debate. Here are the arguments adapted for the case of future bias:

Arbitrariness

1) *Nonarbitrariness:* At any given time, a rational agent's preferences are insensitive to arbitrary differences.
2) Whether an experience happens in the past or the future is an arbitrary difference between them.
3) An agent who exhibits future bias has preferences that are sensitive to whether an experience happens in the past or the future.
4) So, future bias is irrational.

Prudence

1) Rationality requires that an agent prefer outcomes that are in their self-interest over those that are not.
2) An agent with future bias prefers outcomes that are not in their self-interest over those that are.
3) So, future bias is irrational.

If one rejects the arbitrariness and prudence arguments even against uncentered time bias, for instance on permissivist Humean grounds, then one will reject these versions of the arguments for the same reasons. But if one takes the commonsense view that uncentered time bias is irrational for these reasons while defending future bias, special purpose ammunition is required.

Future Bias and the Metaphysics of Time

The natural place to press the arbitrariness argument is once again the second premise. It certainly seems to many people like past and future experiences are different in some normatively significant way. But what is this difference? There are at least two natural ways to try and answer this question. First, we might try to identify some relevant *metaphysical asymmetry between the past and the future* as such. Second, we might try to identify a relevant *asymmetry in our relationship between our past and future selves*. We'll consider these in turn.

Reflecting on the first strategy, one asymmetry that immediately springs to mind is that, time travel aside, we have control over the future but not over the past. But this will not do the required work. First, it does not seem reasonable in general to prefer pleasure that one has control over qualitatively identical pleasure that one doesn't have control over. Moreover, we only have control over *some* future events, but we prefer that pleasurable events are in the future whether or not we have control over them.[29]

A number of philosophers have observed that the prospects for challenging the arbitrariness of future bias rests in part on the true view about the metaphysics of time. We can roughly break views of time into two camps. According to the *Dynamic View*, there are irreducible *tensed* properties or facts – events are objectively future, present, or past, and as time passes they approach from the future and recede into the past. On the dynamic view, the "flow" of time is a metaphysically significant feature of the world. According to the *Static View*, by contrast, there are no irreducible tensed facts – particular events simply occur before or after other events along the dimension of time, which is just one dimension of a four-dimensional spacetime manifold. To say some events are past and some are future is just to say they are on one side of the speaker in the time dimension, just as some objects are to the speaker's left or the speaker's right in space. To say things change as time flows, if it means anything at all, is just to say that things at one temporal location are different than things at other temporal locations – something like suggesting that a rainbow "flows" from one color to another along the spatial dimension.[30]

Since Prior (1959), many philosophers have drawn a connection between future bias and the dynamic view. The reason is straightforward – if the static view is true, then there is no deep metaphysical distinction between the past and

---

[29] Though some, for example Callender and Suhler (2012), Greene and Sullivan (2015), have argued that this control factor is at least *psychologically* explanatory.

[30] The dynamic and static views correspond to what McTaggart (1908) influentially labeled the "A Theory" and "B Theory" of time respectively.

the future – any particular event is past relative to some events and future relative to other events. Caring more about the future than the past is akin to caring more about what happens to your left rather than to your right, which seems paradigmatically arbitrary. Only the dynamic view leaves enough room for the past/future distinction to carry enough metaphysical weight to justify something like future bias.

However, merely introducing a distinction doesn't *explain* why this distinction matters. And unfortunately for this strategy, it is hard to find a plausible explanation. Here it is helpful to look at some subvarieties of dynamic view, which grant additional ontological significance to the past/present/future distinction. One common view, *Presentism*, holds that only present objects exist. Neither past nor future are real (they only *were* real or *will* be real). This might make sense of preferring that pains be in the past rather than the present. But it doesn't justify preferring that pains be in the past rather than the future – since they are equally unreal. Another view is the *Moving Spotlight* theory, on which all of reality exists, but the present is special and active in a way the past and future are not. Again, such a view draws no distinction between the past and the future. A third common view is the *Growing Block* theory (which we have discussed earlier in a different context) – according to that view, the past and the present are real, but the future is not – reality is a four-dimensional block that grows as time passes. But again, this does not vindicate future bias – if anything, it should support a preference that pleasure be in the past (where it actually exists) rather than the future (where it does not).

The view that looks like it would have the best chance of justifying future bias is the *Shrinking Block View*, according to which the future and the present exist, but the past does not. If reality is a shrinking block, then my future pleasure and pain are real but my past pain and pleasure are not. Perhaps that justifies caring more about them. However, the shrinking block view is held by almost nobody,[31] while the growing block theory has seen a number of independent arguments in its favor.[32]

Even if the shrinking block view is correct, the inference to the rationality of future bias can be attacked. Let us grant that the future exists. Still, there seems to be something *special* about the present. In order to capture this specialness and to avoid certain problems, defenders of the growing block picture have proposed that the past, though real, is in some sense "dead." In particular, only beings in the present are conscious, and only mental states in the present are

---

[31] Casati and Torrengo (2011) are a rare exception who argue that it is at least no worse than the growing block view.

[32] Correia and Rosenkranz (2018) offer a sustained defense.

subjectively experienced.[33] The same sorts of considerations seem to apply to the shrinking block theory as well, which therefore has some reason to claim the future is also dead in the relevant sense. But if the future is dead, then why should the bare *existence* of future pleasures and pains there matter to us now? Surely, pains and pleasures only matter insofar as they are qualitatively experienced by sentient beings.

This discussion suggests an interesting and underexplored possibility. It is plausible that it is reasonable to care more about experiences, which are real and experienced. We argued that this consideration does not justify future bias on any of the major theories of the metaphysics of time. However, it *does* seem to favor *present bias*, a preference that good experiences are in the present. It favors present bias not only given presentism, according to which only present events are real at all, but also according to other dynamic views according to which present mental events are unique in being qualitatively experienced, including versions of the moving spotlight, growing block, and shrinking block view which take non-present times to be in some interesting sense "dead." Present bias is almost never discussed in the literature, or it is assumed to come hand in hand with near bias.[34] Our discussion suggests it has independent plausibility and deserves to be taken more seriously.

We have just been looking for something which pastness and futureness bring with them (in particular, the reality and unreality of events) which might justify future bias, but the prospects look fairly grim. One might claim that this was a mistake all along – the reason to care about future pains is not that future events are more real, or have some other interesting nontemporal metaphysical property. It is simply that they *will* happen, and past events *will not*. But without some further explanation of why the fact that something *will* happen justifies more concern than the fact that it *did* happen, this makes the rationality of future bias into a brute fact, and justified by the force of our intuitions about time bias itself. If we have enough faith in these intuitions, perhaps this is enough, but it is not the independent justification we have been searching for. So while the dynamic view of time might *make room* for the view that the rationality of future bias is grounded in a metaphysical distinction between past and future in a way the static view does not, it does not have much to offer in the manner of deeper explanations.

There is a final reason to worry about the prospects of justifying future bias through an appeal to a metaphysical distinction between the past and the present as such. First, let us distinguish the *objective* future from my *subjective* future.

---

[33] See Braddon-Mitchell (2004) for a problem concerning knowledge of our temporal location, and Forrest (2004) for a response on behalf of the growing block view.

[34] Deng et al. (forthcoming) are an exception, though they focus on the psychology of present bias.

The objective future is what we have been discussing so far – what comes after the current moment in the history of the world. My subjective future, on the other hand, is what comes "later" in my internal psychological life – the sequence of my experiences which is linked by causation and narrative order. In normal cases, an experience is in my subjective future if and only if it is in my objective future. But these can come apart in cases of time travel, and so we can test which kind of future matters. Take the following case:[35]

Back to the Future Operation

Deloreas must undergo a medical operation, which normally takes one painful hour without anesthesia. However, the doctors offer her the option of a new treatment plan: instead of having the operation tomorrow, they can put Deloreas in a time machine which will take her back to the middle ages, and she can undergo the operation then. However, medical technology in the middle ages is worse, so the operation would take two painful hours instead.

If Deloreas travels to the past and has the operation there, her pain will be in the objective past but in her subjective future. Is it rational for her to have the operation in the past? Intuitively, it is not. This suggests that insofar as we care more about the future, we care about the *subjective* future. But whether something is in my subjective future isn't a matter of the temporal structure of the world but of the psychological relationship between different time-slices of myself. So we should look for a justification of future bias in our psychology rather than in the metaphysics of time itself.

It is perhaps dangerous to read too much out of examples using time travel, since it is controversial whether time travel is possible, and whether it is consistent with certain views about the nature of time. But even if time travel is not actually possible for physical or metaphysical reasons, the intuitive responses of people who *believe* it is possible can still be relevant evidence for what we take to be normatively relevant. Now, it may be that the bias towards the objective future is the justified one and our intuitive sensitivity to the subjective future is a mistake. But given what we have seen so far about the underwhelming potential of the appeal to the metaphysics of time, this is at least some reason to look elsewhere.

Psychological Connectedness and Future Bias

The fact that our favorable intuitions about future bias seem sensitive to the agent's *subjective* future suggests that we should investigate the psychological relationships with my past and my future self for clues about the justification of

---

[35] Similar cases are discussed by Miller (2021) and Karhu (2022) to make the same point.

future bias. And we saw a very similar strategy employed earlier (though, I suggested, with limited success) in service of near bias. This might raise the hope that we could kill two birds with one stone, and give a unified justification of both future and near bias – a way to deny premise 2 in the arbitrariness argument and premise 1 in the argument from prudence.

However, closer inspection casts doubt on this hope. Most of the connections appealed to by the Parfitian discounting view we discussed earlier will be of little help in justifying future bias, because my past is not consistently less connected to me in the relevant sense than my future. I share beliefs, values, common memories, and the like to a similar degree with my recent past time-slices as with my nearby future time-slices. So these kinds of connections are not asymmetric enough to ground future bias.

Dorsey's appeal to partiality and the bonds of concern, if it justifies any asymmetry between past and future at all, justifies it in the wrong direction. For it seems *easier* to have relationships with my past selves of the kind that plausibly justifies partial concern for others than to future selves. If nothing else, I am better acquainted with my past selves than my future selves, who are more like strangers to me. And my past selves have done things for me for which I might be grateful. Thomas Douglas (2019) has argued, in a paper on parental partiality, that the best grounds for partiality towards our children do not apply to children who are not yet born, precisely because we cannot yet have had the right kinds of experiences with or relationships to them which justify that partiality. The same worries will apply to an attempt to generalize interpersonal reasons of partiality to the relationship between me and my future time-slices.

What we need to make this strategy work is a psychological relationship, which is asymmetric between past and future selves and which plausibly provides a reason to favor the latter. Karhu (2022) proposes such a relationship – *counterfactual and causal dependence*. The experiences and other mental states of my future self depend on mine. But my experiences and other mental states do not depend on theirs.

This is a genuine asymmetry. But that is not enough – this asymmetry needs to be plausible as a grounds for increased concern. And it is hard to see why this would matter in the right way. Note that there are two sides to causal dependence, each equally asymmetric. My mental states *cause* those of my future self. My mental states *are caused* by those of my past self. Why should the relationship of causing someone's mental states motivate caring more about their welfare, while the relationship of being caused by their mental states does not? One thing the Parfitian can say about general psychological connectedness is that those who are more closely connected to me are in some sense "more me" than those who are more distantly connected. But this kind of move is not available here – identity is symmetric, so it does not make sense to say my future self is "more me" than my past self.

Thinking about interpersonal cases can sometimes be illuminating, but here again they do not seem to favor Karhu's story. My students have beliefs which are caused by mine, while my teachers have beliefs which cause mine. But this doesn't seem to be a good reason to favor the interests of my students over the interests of my teachers. Of course, the way in which my future self's mental life depends on mine is much more intimate than the relationship between the beliefs of teachers and students, and so we shouldn't immediately draw any conclusions from the interpersonal case. But we are grasping for any indication of why the causal dependence relation would justify partial concern in one direction only and failing to come up with anything.

Dialectically, then, we are in a similar position as we found ourselves at the end of our exploration of the dynamic view of time. On the dynamic view, there is a metaphysical distinction between futureness and pastness. But we were at a loss to explain why futureness would justify greater concern. Here, similarly, we found an asymmetry in the relationship between us and those time-slices of us in our personal future vs. our personal past. But we are likewise at a loss why the relationship we have to our future selves should make their welfare matter more.

Once again, then, the special resources it seemed like future bias might have against the arguments from bias and prudence have largely evaporated, and we are left little better-off than we would be defending uncentered time bias.

Future Bias and Action

The most salient cases of future bias, like *Past or Future Operation*, describe ways this bias affects our attitudes – what agents should *hope for* or *fear*. In this way it is unlike near bias, which paradigmatically affects people's *choices* in addition to their other attitudes. It is challenging to argue that the manifestation of future bias in attitudes like hope is unreasonable, partly because the intuitions favoring future bias in these attitudes are so strong, but also, one might suspect, because merely having these attitudes, when they do not affect your actions, is so low stakes. It is often assumed that this is inevitable – that there is no way that future bias affects the rationality of actions at all. As Moller (2002) puts it:

> the bias toward the future is essentially a matter of our attitudes and not our actions. This is because our bias involves a contrast between events in the past and the future, and there is no way to act so as to choose the worse of two options just because the one is in the past and the other in the future. (We can only make practical choices about events that are present or future.) (77)

As a consequence, one might think that there cannot be arguments against future bias analogous to the exploitation arguments against near bias, which crucially involved preferences that had practical import, leading agents to make objectionable patterns of decisions. However, several philosophers have tried to come up with clever ways in which, at least for certain kinds of agents, future bias can affect which actions those agents perform, allowing the possibility of arguing that future bias is irrational in virtue of recommending irrational behavior.

Exploitation and Risk-Aversion

Tom Dougherty (2011) has argued that future-biased agents will behave differently from neutral agents as long as they are *risk-averse*. What is important about risk-aversion for his argument is the following: An agent who is risk-averse and facing a 50–50 gamble is always willing to sacrifice something to reduce the gap between the good and the bad outcome by improving the bad outcome and diminishing the good outcome by the same amount. For example, a risk-averse agent facing a gamble between zero units of pleasure and ten units of pleasure would pay some amount to instead face a gamble between one unit and nine units.

For a version of Dougherty's argument, consider *Past and Future Operation* one more time. Dolores, recall, faces the prospect of a two-hour operation on Monday or a one-hour operation on Wednesday. Suppose each outcome is 50 percent likely. Imagine Dolores is risk-averse, and that she is offered an unpleasant-tasting pill which will increase the pain duration of a Wednesday operation by ten minutes and decrease the pain duration of a Monday operation by ten minutes. Since she is risk-averse and this would reduce the gap between the good and bad outcome by the same amount, she will take this pill, as long as the unpleasant taste is mild enough.

Now suppose Tuesday comes along and Dolores wakes up – with amnesia, so she is still 50–50 on whether the operation was on Monday or will be on Wednesday. Now she is offered a second unpleasant-tasting pill. This pill will decrease the pain of the potential Wednesday operation by ten minutes. But if she has already undergone the Monday operation, she will instead experience a bad side effect on Wednesday which will cause her ten minutes of equivalent pain. Assuming she is future-biased, she does not care about her past pain. So again, she will pay some cost to reduce the gap between the worst outcome from her current perspective (having an upcoming operation on Wednesday) and the best (having already had the operation on Monday) by the same amount. So she will take the second pill, as long as the unpleasant taste is mild enough.

But notice that Dolores has taken two unpleasant-tasting pills which otherwise have not reduced her total suffering at all, no matter which operation she was scheduled for. This is worse, both from her earlier and her later perspectives, than if she had taken neither pill. In other words, she has been predictably exploited.

As we saw with the exploitability arguments against non-exponential near bias, there is an additional step a defender of this argument must take in order to bridge the gap between exploitability and irrationality, and there are a couple of options:

1) A future-biased risk-averse agent is exploitable.
2) It is irrational to be exploitable.
3) So, a future-biased risk-averse agent is irrational.

Or:

1) A future-biased risk-averse agent is rationally committed to endorsing preferences which render them exploitable.
2) It is irrational to endorse preferences which render you exploitable.
3) So, a future-biased risk-averse agent is irrational.

Depending on which version we prefer, these arguments will face similar challenges as the analogous arguments against near bias. In the first case, we have the familiar worries about whether exploitability guarantees irrationality, including the attacks on diachronic norms from the time-slice view of rationality and the worries about overgeneralization to changing preferences. In the second case, we require an account of "rational endorsement" which vindicates the premises of the argument. Again, rational endorsement arguably cannot be desire, since a future-biased agent does not seem committed to *wanting* her past self to be biased in this way, and it arguably cannot be a belief about rationality, because this would implausibly imply that believing that changing preferences is rational is irrational.

But there is a new source of worry. So far, the conclusion we have reached is that being future-biased *and* risk-averse is irrational. But what we wanted was an argument that being future-biased by itself was irrational. One might escape this by claiming either that risk-aversion itself is irrational, or that risk-aversion and future bias are irrational *in combination* even though they are not irrational in isolation. So to complete the argument, we must continue:

4) A future-biased risk-averse agent is irrational.
5) If a future-biased risk-averse agent is irrational, then either future bias is irrational or risk-aversion is irrational.
6) Risk-aversion is not irrational
7) So, future bias is irrational.

There is considerable debate over the rationality of risk-aversion in general which we cannot fully consider here, besides noting that it is a matter of controversy and therefore a rickety foundation on which to build an argument against future bias. Greene and Sullivan (2015) make a more narrow argument – that risk-aversion specifically with respect to pleasure and pain would be irrational, on the standard interpretation of risk-averse agents. If that's right, it would at least generate a presumption in against the risk-aversion Dougherty appeals to. However, I think their argument rests on a mistake.

They point out that according to standard rational choice theory as commonly used in economics and decision theory, rational agents always maximize *expected* utility – the sum of the chances of each outcome multiplied by their utility. On this picture, rational agents are *never* risk-averse when it comes to utility itself, and so when they look like they're avoiding risks, this must ultimately be explained by the utility assigned to different outcomes. So, Greene and Sullivan suggest, if they are preferring a guaranteed intermediate pain to an even gamble between no pain at all and double that pain, they are treating the double pain as contributing more than twice the negative utility, and therefore disvaluing that pain more than twice as much. But twice as much pain is twice as bad, and the agent's valuing attitudes should respect this, so this way of disvaluing pain is irrational.

But I think this is too quick a dismissal. First, it is not so obvious that there is something irrational about this pattern of disvalue. That will depend on the prospects of substantive rational constraints on preferences requiring agents to desire things in proportion to their objective value (or, as in the prudence argument, in proportion to how good they are for the agent). But more importantly, we should not assume that risk-aversion is explained via the way the agent values outcomes.

We should not assume this in part because there are serious accounts of rational risk-aversion that depart from standard rational choice theory (Buchak 2013), as Sullivan and Greene acknowledge but set aside. But what is truly standard even in the standard view does not require thinking that an agent for whom pain has diminishing marginal disutility *values* pain in the way Greene and Sullivan find objectionable.

Borrowing terminology from Hansson (1988), the idea of "utility" in the standard expected utility theory can be given a *realistic* or a *formalistic* interpretation. On the realistic interpretation, an agent's utility function, which assigns numbers to various outcomes, represents independent psychological facts about how good outcomes are from the agent's point of view or how strongly she desires them. On the formalistic interpretation, the agent's utilities are just whatever quantities the agent can be modeled as maximizing the expectation of, for the purposes of predicting her choices under uncertainty. Importantly, the formalistic interpretation does not assume that the numbers correspond directly to the agent's valuing or desiring attitudes towards those outcomes, as Greene and Sullivan are assuming. The kind of agent who genuinely disvalues the double pain more than twice as much can be modeled with the same utility function as an agent who has the same behavioral dispositions for different reasons having to do with their attitudes or inclinations regarding risk. In most of the literature, particularly in economics, where the point is to describe and predict behavior, employment of the standard expected utility framework is compatible with a formalistic inter-pretation. So Greene and Sullivan's appeal to the wide use of this framework in support of the irrationality of hedonic risk-aversion is illegitimate.

Exploitation Without Risk-Aversion

Christian Tarsney (2017) has recently argued that future bias has practical relevance even without auxiliary assumptions about risk-aversion. Here is the kind of case he discusses:

Shocking Situation

Tim has been abducted by an evil demon, who has hooked him up to a machine and subjected him over the past several days to a series of thousands of uniformly unpleasant electrical shocks – so many that Tim has lost count. Finally, the demon reveals himself and announces that he will soon let Tim go. But the demon offers Tim a choice before he leaves. He may press the button on the torture machine himself and experience one more shock, or he can refrain from pressing the button. Before Tim makes up his mind, the demon (who we may assume is as honest as he is cruel) gives him one final bit of information: The demon decided how many times to shock Tim over the last few days on the basis of instructions handed to him by one of his minions, who arrived a few days ago in a time machine. And he is, right now, about to send that very minion back in time with those very instructions. If Tim decides to shock himself one last time, the demon will send instructions to shock Tim 10,000 times. If Tim decides not to shock himself one last time, the demon will send back instructions to shock Tim 10,005 times. Since Tim has lost count, he has no idea whether the demon has shocked him 10,000 or 10,005 times.

If Tim is sufficiently future-biased, he will prefer avoiding the future shock even if it means more shocks in the past. If he is neutral, he will instead minimize the total amount of shocks and shock himself one last time. So future bias has an effect on Tim's choices.

Tarsney finds it intuitively reasonable for Tim to refuse the shock, and presents this as a problem for views which deny this. But we can borrow Tarsney's setup to generate something which has evaded us so far – a case of exploitation generated by future bias which does not rely on other independent attitudes the agent has, such as risk-aversion.

A simple way of accomplishing this is by adding to the *Shocking Situation* case an additional detail. Earlier, on the first day of his torture, the demon presents Tim with an initial offer: He will make the next three shocks completely painless, in exchange for painfully shocking Tim twice more several days later, after Tim makes the final decision described in the initial problem. Since two future shocks are better than three, a future-biased Tim will accept this offer. As a result of both of his decisions, then, Tim suffers 10,004 painful shocks: 10,002 before his second decision and two after. But this is worse, both from his earlier perspective and his later perspective, than rejecting the initial offer and then shocking himself once later. He has effectively traded three early shocks for two late shocks, and then one late shock for five early shocks, leaving himself two early shocks and one late shock worse for no benefit. In other words, he has been exploited. If all this is right, we are in a position to give a simpler version of an exploitation argument against future bias:

1) A future-biased agent is exploitable.
2) It is irrational to be exploitable.
3) So, a future-biased agent is irrational.

All of the worries we've already raised about exploitation apply here, of course. Tarsney himself expresses skepticism about exploitation arguments on the basis of the analogy with changing preferences in general – though as we saw, an endorsement version of the exploitation argument might allow us to draw a relevant distinction. One might be additionally worried about the role time travel plays in this example, either because one judges it metaphysically impossible or because one suspects it makes a mess of theories of rational decision-making even aside from issues involving temporal bias. Notably, Tarsney demonstrates in his paper how a similar setup can be achieved without the involvement of time travel, but there is a downside – it requires one to take sides on a decision-theoretic controversy over the infamous *Newcomb Problem* – essentially, a case can be constructed without time travel if *evidential* decision theory is correct, but not if *causal* decision theory is correct.[36] So a causal theorist who also finds time travel examples objectionable will not be convinced. Otherwise, however, this kind of test case relies on fewer assumptions than Dougherty's, and is a cleaner test of the exploitation strategy.

---

[36] Nozick (1969) presents the original problem and lays out the two main responses.

Regret and the Scheduling Problem

Given the worries about the rational import of diachronic exploitability, there would be some advantage to an argument that could show that future-biased agents behave irrationally on particular occasions, and not just that they find themselves exploited over time. Greene and Sullivan (2015) provide an argument with this ambition based on principles surrounding *regret*. They present the following case:

Fine Dining

> Jack wins a free meal at a fancy French restaurant on Monday morning, and he must schedule the meal for a night sometime in the next week. Given his flexible schedule, every night is equally convenient for him, and there are no other considerations that would make the meal more enjoyable or more likely to occur on one night rather than another. Therefore, Jack schedules the meal for Monday night. As expected, it is an incredibly delicious meal. On Tuesday morning, Jack strongly prefers that his restaurant experience were in the future, rather than the past. And so he regrets scheduling the meal for the previous night. (959)

Indeed, Greene and Sullivan argue, Jack will regret scheduling his meal any night except for the very last night it is available. Consequently, if Jack wants to avoid regret, he is forced to delay the meal for the final night, even though it is no better then. But delaying gratification like this, they think, is absurd. They go on to suggest that Jack would be required, even more absurdly, to schedule the meal for the last possible moment even if the experience would be significantly worse then, because otherwise he will regret not delaying once the experience is past and therefore sapped of value from his perspective. They label this the *scheduling problem*.

Just as Dougherty's argument requires the agent to be risk-averse in addition to future-biased before they act in a purportedly objectionable way, Greene and Sullivan require the agent to be *regret-averse*. But they think regret aversion is rational, endorsing it in the form of the thesis: "If an agent has full and accurate information about the effects of the options available to her, then it is rationally permissible for her to avoid options she knows she will regret in favor of ones she knows she will never regret." (958) The full argument, then, would look something like the following:

1) If an agent is future-biased, then she will regret scheduling a good experience before the last possible moment, even if the experience would be worse.

2) If an agent is future-biased, then she will not regret scheduling a good experience at the last possible moment.

3) It is not rational for an agent to schedule a good experience at the last possible moment.
4) So, a regret-averse future-biased agent is irrational.
5) If a regret-averse future-biased agent is irrational, then either regret aversion is irrational or future bias is irrational.
6) Regret aversion is not irrational.
7) So, future bias is irrational.

This argument has several problems. First, although Greene and Sullivan say premise 2 is true even when the good experience would be worse when it is scheduled later, I think this is false. Jack is facing a decision, in the present, about when to schedule his dinner. If he schedules it before the last moment, Greene and Sullivan are right that he will regret that decision once the dinner is over. But if he schedules it for the last moment, he *also* will regret it – in fact, he will regret it immediately, since right now both experiences are in the future and he has chosen one that is worse over one that is better. Greene and Sullivan seem to be considering regret only from the point *after the dinner has been eaten*. But to make it plausible that regret-free options are rationally preferred, we need to allow regret *starting at the point of decision*. So regrettableness from the agent's current perspective, in which all the events to be scheduled lie in the future, will matter. And this rules out cases where the agent chooses less pleasure later over more pleasure sooner.

Greene and Sullivan could retreat to considering only scheduling cases where the amount of pleasure is the same no matter when it is scheduled. But it is much less obvious then that it is *irrational* for a regret-averse agent to schedule the pleasure late. If every day for Jack's dinner is equally good, and Jack is regret-averse, scheduling it late does not seem so bad. It is important to keep in mind that we are not committed to claiming that *any* rational agent must schedule it late, for Greene and Sullivan posit regret aversion as merely permissible. To give the implications more bite, one could insist that regret aversion is a requirement, but this would make the case substantially harder to make.

Second, and perhaps more fundamentally, the kind of regret-aversion employed by the argument is extremely strong. It should not be confused, for example, for the more plausible claim that it is rationally permissible for someone to care about living a life they don't regret. An agent who cares about regret still weighs that concern against other concerns they have, and might do something they will regret if it realizes other important values of theirs. Sullivan and Greene's regret aversion, on the other hand, requires an agent to treat regret as trumping all other consider-ations. And there are intuitive counterexamples to this. Here is a case discussed by Pettigrew (2019):

Taste Pills

> The scientists at the local Sense Perception Lab have developed two pills. Pill A makes me love lemon sorbet, but love dark chocolate ice cream even more; Pill B makes me hate lemon sorbet, and hate dark chocolate ice cream only slightly less. I am offered two menus when I dine at their cafeteria: Pill A for starter and lemon sorbet for dessert; or Pill B to start and dark chocolate ice cream for dessert. (226)

It's important to clarify that when the pills make you love or hate the dessert, they make you intrinsically desire or be averse to outcomes involving you having it, and not merely affect the pleasure you get from it. Understood this way, the regret-averse agent will pick Pill B, because this is the only option they will not regret. But this means picking something they will hate over something they will love – it is at best far from obvious that this is rational. And indeed, most theories of rational decision-making are not framed retrospectively, in terms of minimizing regret, but in terms of the prospective value of the options from the agent's perspective. Thinking about decisions in terms of avoiding regret, while natural, can plausibly be explained as a heuristic which works well when our relevant preferences over outcomes are expected to be stable over time. When our decisions affect our values, as in Pettigrew's example, and when our preferences over outcomes shift over time, as in cases of future bias, this heuristic may fall apart.

I will end with one positive suggestion for the strategy of criticizing future bias from the point of view of regret. We saw the appeal to the rationality of regret aversion struggle with cases of changing preferences like *Taste Pills*. And we could imagine other cases where you expect to undergo radical changes in your psychology where your future regrets do not seem rationally relevant. Since an agent with a centered time bias such as future bias has, in some sense, changing preferences as well, it might look like we should treat all these cases the same. But we have already seen earlier a promising way to distinguish the preference change involved in centered time biases from other kinds of preference change by appealing to *rational endorsement*.

How could this help? *Taste Pills* suggests that it is not in general rational to minimize regret. But there is something odd about the regret you will feel when you take Pill B – it is regret that is not grounded in anything resembling your current perspective. Given that you don't currently hate lemon sorbet, it is not a regret you *currently endorse*. And in general, if you expect to acquire some bizarre desires in the future, you are not committed to currently endorsing the regrets you will have as a result of those desires. It is more plausible that it is rational to avoid regret *that you are committed to endorsing* than that it is rational to avoid regret full-stop.

We saw some plausibility in our discussion of near bias to the idea that you are rationally committed to endorsing the preferences you would have if you satisfied *Stationarity* – that is, you are committed to endorsing preferences in the future which reflect a centered bias which matches yours. This applies just as well to future bias as near bias – if you are future-biased now, you would be rationally committed to endorsing your later future bias. And this means that we could use narrower principles involving regret and still get a similar argument off the ground – for example "it is rational to choose options you do not endorse ever regretting over options you do endorse regretting." These principles would be more difficult to refute with examples of ordinary preference change, and so I think they would be an improvement over the existing argument.

Conclusion

Our discussion has covered a lot of terrain, so I'll end with a summary of what I take to be the most general lessons, given the evaluations I have defended of the arguments over time bias.

I proposed that the strongest argument against *un*centered time bias (aside, perhaps, from an appeal to raw intuition) was the argument from arbitrariness. And while we looked at several attempts to justify near bias and future bias as *less* arbitrary than uncentered time bias, I argued that these attempts were largely unsuccessful. Neither psychological connectedness nor the bonds of concern provide a convincing ground for near bias, and neither the metaphysics of time nor asymmetric relationships of psychological dependence provide a convincing ground for future bias. This means that a great deal rests on the success or failure of the arbitrariness argument, and that argument depends crucially on the stance one takes about the relationship between substantive reasons and rational desires – particularly on whether a roughly Humean, permissive view is correct.

If my evaluations are right, then there does not seem to be any strong argument that uncentered, near, or future bias are rationally *required*. They are fighting for permissibility at best. On the other hand, there is at least some reason to think a case for *present* bias, largely ignored in the literature, would be more successful. Arguments from intuition and alienation for Parfitian near bias are, I suggested, more plausible as motivations for privileging our present aims, and arguments from the metaphysics of time are much less attractive as justifications of future bias than present bias.

We also looked at a family of arguments which criticized near and future bias for recommending irrational patterns of actions. Standard versions of these arguments must make highly controversial commitments about diachronic rational requirements and about the irrationality of exploitation, and threaten to overgeneralize to preference change in general. I suggested that a promising way to mitigate these problems involves a roughly Kantian appeal to synchronic norms on rational endorsement, though this view faces challenges characterizing the nature of this endorsement. Together with the aforementioned prospects for present bias, this kind of argument warrants deeper exploration.

There are, of course, many aspects of the existing debate over time bias we have not covered. In narrowing our focus to hedonic time bias towards agents' own good, we have skipped over several interesting side plots in the literature, including the prospects for time bias in non-hedonic goods and the relationship between our biases regarding our own pleasure and suffering and that of other people.

Most importantly, we did not consider arguments which appeal to, or which criticize, the bare intuition that certain kinds of time bias are rational or irrational. Those strategies call for engagement with the psychological literature on the sources of our dispositions towards time bias in order to assess the plausibility of debunking explanations if for no other reason. The more convincing one finds refutations of the more theoretical arguments we considered in this Element, the more important this project of interrogating our intuitions will be, and the more it might seem that appropriateness or inappropriateness of time bias is something that must simply be apprehended directly. But even if raw intuitions provide the strongest *justificatory* force favoring one view of time bias over another, I think the kind of deeper explanatory ambitions we've pursued are important. For we can run the arguments in reverse – if the best theoretical justifications of some attitude towards time rely on highly controversial commitments, then our independent confidence in the intuitions favoring that attitude could end up being part of the best arguments for accepting those commitments.

References

Ahmed, A. (2018). Rationality and Future Discounting. *Topoi*, 39(2), 245–256.

Ainslie, G. & Haslam, N. (1992). Hyperbolic Discounting. In G. Loewenstein & J. Elster (eds.), *Choice Over Time*. Russell Sage Foundation, 57–92.

Baker, C. & Maguire, B. (2020). The Alienation Objection to Consequentialism. In *Oxford Handbook of Consequentialism*. Oxford University Press, 477–491.

Braddon-Mitchell, D. (2004). How Do We Know It Is Now Now? *Analysis*, 64, 199–203.

Bransen, J. (2015). Self-Knowledge and Self-Love. *Ethical Theory and Moral Practice*, 18(2), 309–321.

Brink, D. O. (2011). Prospects for Temporal Neutrality. In Craig Callender (ed.), *Oxford Handbook of Philosophy of Time*. Oxford University Press, 353–381.

Broome, J. (2013). *Rationality through Reasoning*. Wiley-Blackwell.

Buchak, L. (2013). *Risk and Rationality*. Oxford University Press.

Callender, C. (2023). Temporal Neutrality Implies Exponential Temporal Discounting. *Philosophy of Science*. Advance Online Publication.

Callender, C. & Suhler, C. (2012). Thank Goodness That Argument Is Over: Explaining the Temporal Value Asymmetry. *Philosophers' Imprint*, 12, 1–16.

Caruso, E. M., Gilbert, D. T., & Wilson, T. D. (2008). A Wrinkle in Time Asymmetric Valuation of Past and Future Events. *Psychological Science*, 19(8), 796–801.

Casati, R. & Torrengo, G. (2011). The Not So Incredible Shrinking Future. *Analysis*, 71(2), 240–244.

Caspar, H. (2013). Time – The Emotional Asymmetry. In Heather Dyke & Adrian Bardon (eds.), *A Companion to the Philosophy of Time*. Chichester, UK: Wiley, 507–520.

Charvet, J. (1995). *The Idea of an Ethical Community*. Cornell University Press.

Christensen, D. (1996). Dutch-Book Arguments Depragmatized: Epistemic Consistency for Partial Believers. *Journal of Philosophy*, 93(9), 450–479.

Correia, F. & Rosenkranz, S. (2018). Nothing to Come: A Defence of the Growing Block Theory of Time. Springer.

Deng, N., Latham, A. J., Miller, K., & Norton, J. (forthcoming). There's No Time Like the Present: Present-Bias, Temporal Attitudes and Temporal Ontology. In J. Knobe and S. Nichols (eds.), *Oxford Studies in Experimental Philosophy*. Oxford University Press.

Dorsey, D. (2019). A Near-Term Bias Reconsidered. *Philosophy and Phenomenological Research*, 99(2), 461–477.

Dougherty, T. (2011). On Whether to Prefer Pain to Pass. *Ethics*, 121(3), 521–537.

Dougherty, T. (2015). Future Bias and Practical Reason. *Philosophers' Imprint*, 15.

Douglas, T. (2019). Parental Partiality and Future Children. *Journal of Ethics and Social Philosophy*, 15(1), 1–18.

Ericson, K. M. & Laibson, D. (2019). Intertemporal Choice. In B. D. Bernheim, S. DellaVigna, & D. Laibson, (eds.), *Handbook of Behavioral Economics: Applications and Foundations*, Vol. 2, chapter 1. Elsevier, 1–67.

Forrest, P. (2004). The Real but Dead Past: A Reply to Braddon-Mitchell. *Analysis*, 64(4), 358–362.

Frederick, S., Loewenstein, G., & O'Donoghue, T. (2002). Time Discounting and Time Preference: A Critical Review. *Journal of Economic Literature*, 40(2), 351–401.

Greene, P. & Sullivan, M. (2015). Against Time Bias. *Ethics*, 125(4), 947–970.

Greene, P., Latham, A. J., Miller, K., & Norton, J. (2022). Capacity for Simulation and Mitigation Drives Hedonic and Non-hedonic Time Biases. *Philosophical Psychology*, 35(2), 226–252.

Gustafsson, J. (2022). *Money-Pump Arguments*. Cambridge University Press.

Halevy, Y. (2015). Time Consistency: Stationarity and Time Invariance. *Econometrica*, 83(1), 335–352.

Hansson, B. (1988). Risk-Aversion as a Problem of Conjoint Measurement. In P. Gärdenfors and N.-E. Sahlin (eds.), *Decision, Probability, and Utility*. Cambridge University Press, 136–158.

Hare, C. (2007). Self-Bias, Time-Bias, and the Metaphysics of the Self and Time. *Journal of Philosophy*, 104(7), 350–373.

Hare, C. (2008). A Puzzle about Other-Directed Time-Bias. *Australasian Journal of Philosophy*, 86(2), 269–277.

Heathwood, C. (2008). Fitting Attitudes and Welfare. *Oxford Studies in Metaethics*, 3, 47–73.

Heathwood, C. (2016). Desire-Fulfillment Theory. In G. Fletcher (ed.), *The Routledge Handbook of the Philosophy of Well-Being*. Routledge, 135–147.

Heathwood, C. (2019). Which Desires Are Relevant to Well-Being? *Noûs*, 53(3), 664–688.

Hedden, B. (2015a). Time-Slice Rationality. *Mind*, 124(494), 449–491.

Hedden, B. (2015b). Options and Diachronic Tragedy. *Philosophy and Phenomenological Research*, 90(2), 423–451.

Hedden, B. (2016). Does MITE Make Right?: On Decision-Making under Normative Uncertainty. In R. Shafer-Landau (ed.), *Oxford Studies in Metaethics*, 11, 102–128.

Hubin, D. (1991). Irrational Desires. *Philosophical Studies*, 62(1), 23–44.

Hume, D. (1739). *A Treatise of Human Nature*. Oxford University Press.

Kagan, S. (1986). The Present-Aim Theory of Rationality. *Ethics*, 96(4), 746–759.

Kahneman, D., Fredrickson, B. L., Schreiber C. A., & Redelmeier D. A. (1993). When More Pain Is Preferred to Less: Adding a Better End. *Psychological Science*, 4(6), 401–405.

Karhu, T. (2022). What Justifies Our Bias toward the Future? *Australasian Journal of Philosophy*. Advance online publication.

Keller, S. (2006). Four Theories of Filial Duty. *The Philosophical Quarterly*, 56(223), 254–274.

Kiesewetter, B. (2020). Rationality as Reasons-Responsiveness. *Australasian Philosophical Review*, 4(4), 332–342.

Korsgaard, C. M. (1985). Kant's Formula of Universal Law. *Pacific Philosophical Quarterly*, 66(1–2), 24–47.

Latham, A. J., Miller, K., & Norton, J. (2023). Against a Normative Asymmetry between Near- and Future-Bias. *Synthese*, 201(3), 1–31.

Levi, I. (2002). Money Pumps and Diachronic Books. *Philosophy of Science*, 69(3), 235–247.

Loewenstein, G. & Prelec, D. (1993). Preferences for Sequences of Outcomes. *Psychological Review*, 100(1), 91–108.

Lowry, R. & Peterson, M. (2011). Pure Time Preference. *Pacific Philosophical Quarterly*, 92(4), 490–508.

McMahan, J. (2002). *The Ethics of Killing: Problems at the Margins of Life*. Oxford University Press.

McTaggart, J. M. E. (1908). The Unreality of Time. *Mind*, 17, 457–474.

Miller, K. (2021). What Time-Travel Teaches Us about Future-Bias. *Philosophies*, 6(38), 1–18.

Moller, D. (2002). Parfit on Pains, Pleasures, and the Time of Their Occurrence. *Canadian Journal of Philosophy*, 32(1), 67–82.

Nozick, R. (1969). Newcomb's Problem and Two Principles of Choice. In N. Rescher (ed.), *Essays in Honor of Carl G. Hempel*. Reidel, 114–146.

Parfit, Derek. (1984). *Reasons and Persons*. Oxford University Press.

Paul, L. (2014). *Transformative Experience*. Oxford University Press.

Pettigrew, R. (2019). *Choosing for Changing Selves*. Oxford University Press.

Pettigrew, R. (2020). *Dutch Book Arguments*. Cambridge University Press.

Pigou, A. C. (1920). *The Economics of Welfare*. Macmillan.

Plato. (1992). *Protagoras*. Translated by Lombardo, S., & Bell, K. Hackett.

Podgorski, A. (2016). A Reply to the Synchronist. *Mind*, 125(499), 859–871.

Prior, A. (1959). Thank Goodness That's over. *Philosophy*, 34(128), 12–17.

Railton, P. (1984). Alienation, Consequentialism, and the Demands of Morality. *Philosophy & Public Affairs*, 13(2), 134–171.

Saad, B. (2023). The Sooner the Better: An Argument for Bias toward the Earlier. *Journal of the American Philosophical Association*.

Sidgwick, H. (1884). *The Methods of Ethics*. Macmillan.

Street, S. (2009). In Defense of Future Tuesday Indifference: Ideally Coherent Eccentrics and the Contingency of What Matters. *Philosophical Issues*, 19(1), 273–298.

Strotz, R. H. (1955). Myopia and Inconsistency in Dynamic Utility Maximization. *The Review of Economic Studies*, 23(3), 165–180.

Sullivan, M. (2018). *Time Biases: A Theory of Rational Planning and Personal Persistence*. Oxford University Press.

Tarsney, C. (2017). Thank Goodness that's Newcomb: The Practical Relevance of the Temporal Value Asymmetry. *Analysis*, 77(4), 750–759.

Titelbaum, M. G. (2015). Rationality's Fixed Point (or: In Defense of Right Reason). In T. Szabó Gendler and John Hawthorne (eds.), *Oxford Studies in Epistemology*, Volume 5. Oxford University Press, 253–294.

Urminsky, O. (2017). The Role of Psychological Connectedness to the Future Self in Decisions over Time. *Current Directions in Psychological Science*, 26(1), 34–39.

Velleman, J. D. (1991). Well-Being and Time. *Pacific Philosophical Quarterly*, 72(1), 48–77.

Wang, M., Rieger, M. O., & Hens, T. (2016). How Time Preferences Differ: Evidence from 53 Countries. *Journal of Economic Psychology*, 52, 115–135.

Weatherson, B. (2019). *Normative Externalism*. Oxford University Press.

Żuradzki, T. (2016). Time-Biases and Rationality: The Philosophical Perspectives on Empirical Research about Time Preferences. In J. Stelmach, B. Brożek, & Ł. Kurek (eds.), *The Emergence of Normative Orders*. Copernicus Press, 149–187.

Cambridge Elements ☰

Decision Theory and Philosophy

Martin Peterson

Texas A&M University

Martin Peterson is Professor of Philosophy and Sue and Harry E. Bovay Professor of the History and Ethics of Professional Engineering at Texas A&M University. He is the author of four books and one edited collection, as well as many articles on decision theory, ethics and philosophy of science.

About the Series

This Cambridge Elements series offers an extensive overview of decision theory in its many and varied forms. Distinguished authors provide an up-to-date summary of the results of current research in their fields and give their own take on what they believe are the most significant debates influencing research, drawing original conclusions.

Cambridge Elements ☰

Decision Theory and Philosophy

Elements in the Series

A full series listing is available at: www.cambridge.org/EDTP